The Complete
ARCHERY
Book

by Louis Hochman

New York

Published by ARCO PUBLISHING COMPANY, Inc.
219 Park Avenue South, New York, N.Y. 10003

Second Printing, 1975

Library of Congress Catalog Card Number 57-2516

ISBN 0-668-00552-1

Printed in the United States of America

Cover and all other photos by the
author, unless otherwise credited.

Grateful acknowledgment is made to the following organiza-
tions for cooperation and assistance in the preparation of this
book: Smithwick Archery, North Hollywood, Calif.; Shawnee
Archery, Sunland, Calif.; Ken Cooper's Sportsman's Haven,
Encino, Calif.; Hugh Rich Archery Co., Glendale, Calif.; Pro
Archery Shop, Costa Mesa, Calif.; Dee's Archery, Upland,
Calif.; Joe Fries Archery, Los Angeles, Calif.; charter boat
"Pappy," Bill Carpenter, operator, Newport Beach, Calif.;
National Field Archery Association, Redlands, Calif.; Southern
California Field Archery Association, Los Angeles, Calif.;
National Archery Association, Amherst, Mass.; National Com-
pany of Crossbowmen, Coronado, Calif.; Wamo Manufacturing
Co., San Gabriel, Calif.

CONTENTS

INTRODUCTION

Archery is the romantic sport, steeped in colorful legend, glorified in poem and song, instrument of the immortal matchmaker, Cupid, and joy of countless modern archers who thrill to the twang of the bowstring and the sight of the arrow target-bound. Each year, the ranks of organized archery swell to new proportions as enthusiasts in every age bracket join the many clubs and associations devoted to the sport. Archery is the ideal family sport, combining the thrills of competitive skill for young and old, male and female alike, with the pleasures and benefits of healthy outdoor living.

As a hunting weapon, the bow and arrow is more sporting than the gun, killing cleaner and more quietly, yet giving the animal every possible advantage in the field. The bow-hunter who downs his quarry demonstrates a hunting skill he can be proud of, for it takes infinitely more skill to hunt successfully with bow and arrow than it does with a gun.

To give the reader — beginner and skilled archer alike — the most up-to-date fund of practical archery information and know-how possible, I sought and received the help of many of the top people in archery — people like Howard Hill, the great bowhunter; Joe Fries, National Target Champ; Jo McCubbins, National Women's Instinctive Champ; Ken Cooper, archery instructor; Hugh Rich, president of the Southern California Field Archery Association; Bob Markworth, and many, many others. Here for the first time in print are their "trade" secrets, unselfishly revealed in the interests of archery, plus detailed instructions on making and using equipment that will benefit every archer.

The Mechanics of the Bow

Modern science has been responsible for perfecting today's bow,
making it superior in every way to its ancestral predecessors.

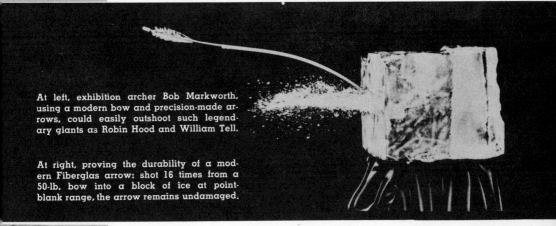

At left, exhibition archer Bob Markworth, using a modern bow and precision-made arrows, could easily outshoot such legendary giants as Robin Hood and William Tell.

At right, proving the durability of a modern Fiberglas arrow: shot 16 times from a 50-lb. bow into a block of ice at point-blank range, the arrow remains undamaged.

Courtesy Paul Bunyan Archery

THOUGH man has been using the bow and arrow for many, many centuries, it is only in fairly recent times that he has actually come to understand the mechanics of this ancient weapon. Primitive man knew only that it could hurl a barbed shaft with deadly force, so he developed his stalking talents to the point where he could get close enough to his prey to insure a hit in spite of poor marksmanship. The American Indian was a notoriously bad shot, but he made up for this with his uncanny stalking ability. The idea of individually aimed fire wasn't even considered in ancient times, the bow and arrow being used mainly as a saturation weapon. The strategy of warring archers was to shoot volleys, to "fill the sky with arrows," and trust to luck that enough of them would find a mark to turn the tide of battle.

The ancient Asiatics of early recorded history used composite, reflexed bows of wood, horn and sinew that weighed up to 100 pounds. Great Britain won supremacy on the battlefield with the six-foot longbow, and the legendary feats of William Tell and Robin Hood added to the lore of archery. But it remained for modern science to delve into the physics of archery and show us just what makes a bow flex and an arrow fly. This knowledge, gained by slide rule, high-speed stroboscopic photography, and other super-scientific instruments and devices, has been responsible for the perfecting of the modern bow, which is far superior in every way to its ancestral predecessors. The archer who understands the physics of archery is better equipped to enjoy his sport and become a better archer.

Basically, the shooting power of a bow is derived from the tendency of its limbs to return to normal after they have been pulled into a flexed curve. The faster the limbs return to normal, the faster and farther the arrow will fly. The factors that govern the speed (or cast) of a bow are (1) its design, (2) the materials it is made of, and (3) the stiffness of the limbs.

Design-wise, there are three basic bows: the straight-end bow, the static recurve, and the working recurve. In between these are a variety of modifications, like the semi-recurve, the semi-working recurve, the longbow, the short bow, etc., each designed with the idea of combining the best features of the various designs minus their inherent faults.

As mentioned above, the shooting power of the bow is derived from the tendency of its flexed limbs to return to normal when released. The faster this return is effected, the more speed or cast

5

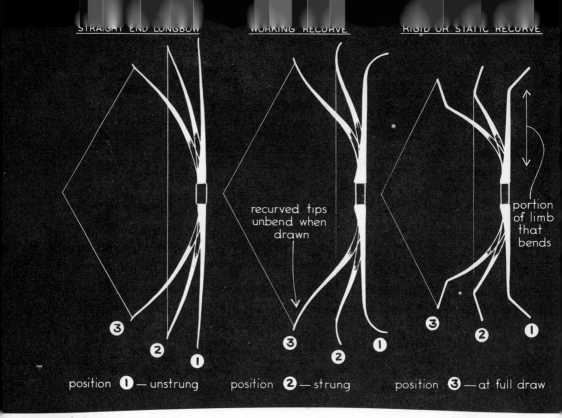

recurved tips
unbend when
drawn

portion
of limb
that
bends

position **1**—unstrung   position **2**—strung   position **3**—at full draw

the bow will have. The two basic factors that will increase the speed of a flexed limb's return to normal are (1) the stiffness of the limb, and (2) the degree to which it is flexed. The stiffer the limb, the faster it will return, and likewise, the more it is bent without overstraining its fibers, the faster it will return.

Limb stiffness is achieved by one or all of three means: increasing the width of the limb, its thickness, and/or decreasing its length. Double the width of a limb and you double its stiffness, but double its thickness and you increase its stiffness by a factor of two cubed, or eight. Thus, by adding to the thickness of a limb, you can make it considerably stiffer than by merely adding to its width.

Shortening the length of a limb by 10 percent will increase its stiffness by 11 percent, provided, of course, the limb is equal in thickness and width throughout its entire length.

Finally, the more you bend a limb, the faster it will return. This is the principle on which all of the various recurve designs are based. By designing a bow with its limbs curved back away from the handle when unstrung, the limbs must be pulled into considerable tension just to bring them

into strung position. From this pre-flexed position, they are flexed even more when brought to full-draw position. It is easy to see how much more tension is exerted on a bow of this reflex design than on a straight-end bow which begins its flexing from a normal perpendicular position.

The straight-end bow, because of its simplicity of design and function, is a more stable and dependable bow than the recurve, but it lacks the speed and efficiency of the recurve. In order to gain more speed with a straight-end bow, it must be made stiffer and hence requires more strength to pull. Because of this, the straight-end bow has become more or less obsolete among serious archers who prefer the recurves for their target and hunting activities.

The static recurve is a bow with limb tips curved back away from the handle, often at a fairly sharp angle. This curve is rigid and does not unbend as the limb is flexed. Its function is to provide leverage for the string, allowing a stiffer limb to be bent with less muscular effort expended in the process. In effect, it is actually a short bow with longbow handling characteristics, since the portion of the limbs that bend are only the short lengths between the handle and the start of the recurves. A short bow

SHORT BOW

short bow cuts down
string angle and
pinches fingers

LONG BOW

long bow has wider string angle,
smoother cast than short bow

without the recurved tips would require considerably more effort to pull, and the resultant short angle of the string at full draw would cramp the draw fingers, producing "string pinch" and making a smooth release very difficult. This is one of the faults of the short bow.

The working recurve is similar to the static recurve in design, with the exception that the tips take a more graceful curve and are not rigid. When the bow is drawn, the curved tips unbend, like an unwinding spring. Upon release, they snap forward, adding an initial thrust to the force of the relaxing limbs. This not only increases the cast of the bow but also makes for smoother operation. The bow is easier to draw and does not have a tendency to stack up at the end of the draw; that is, draw easily for the first two thirds of the draw, then become a disproportionate strain for the last third of the draw. A bow can easily be checked for this characteristic by weighing it and noting how gradually or abruptly its weight increases toward the end of the draw.

Aside from the design of the bow, a vital

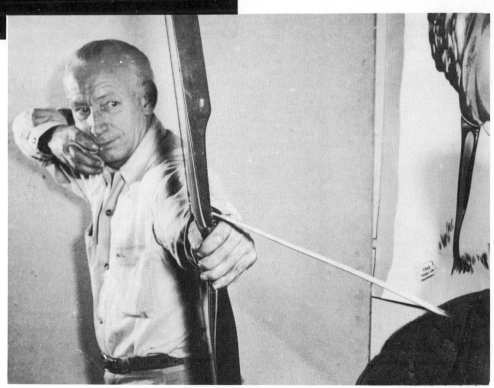

High-speed-strobe photo of arrow just leaving the bow catches oscillation of the arrow. The arrow is just straightening out after bending around the bow. This phenomenon is known as the archer's paradox.

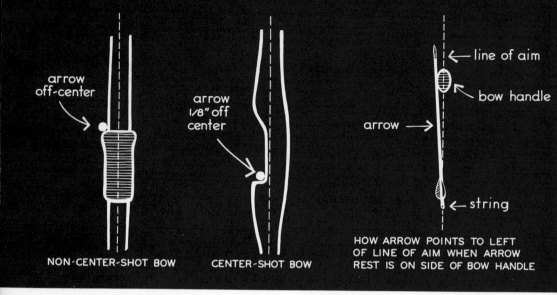

arrow
off-center

arrow
1/8" off
center

← line of aim

← bow handle

arrow →

← string

NON-CENTER-SHOT BOW

CENTER-SHOT BOW

HOW ARROW POINTS TO LEFT
OF LINE OF AIM WHEN ARROW
REST IS ON SIDE OF BOW HANDLE

factor in its tensile characteristics is its physical composition. When a limb bends, it undergoes a combination of opposing stresses and strains which fight to return it to its original relaxed shape. The back of the bow stretches by tension and the belly becomes shorter by compression. In between these two outer surfaces, there lies an inner neutral core or line along which there is no stress. Upon release, this combination of tension and compression forces the limbs to snap back to their original shape. The more tension and compression a material can withstand, the better suited it is to bow-making. Over the centuries, bows have been laminated with such materials as bone, sinew, horn, plastic, bamboo, aluminum, and now, Fiberglas.

Today, high-quality Fiberglas, made especially for bows, is the material used in the better bows. Its high tensile and compression characteristics give the bow 88 percent of its active power, the wood laminations serving only as the neutral core and carrying just 12 percent of the load.

The solid center section of the bow also serves the functional purpose of absorbing the shock of the bow into the handle without transmitting it to the bow hand.

When an arrow is shot from a bow, theoretically it should fly off to the left, since it passes along the left side of the bow handle while the released string returns to the center of the bow. However, with an arrow of the correct stiffness or spine for the bow weight, this is not true, for the arrow, under sudden and terrific pressure from the string, actually buckles around the bow handle and straightens out

in flight to follow a course along the line of aim instead of going off to the left as its position on the bow would indicate. This phenomena is known as the archer's paradox and is the reason why such care must be taken to match the spine of the arrow to the drawing weight of the bow being used. If an arrow is too stiff for the bow, it will not bend sufficiently around the bow handle and hence will fly off to the left. On the other hand, an arrow that is too weak in spine will buckle too much and fly off to the right. Although the required spine of an arrow is generally determined by the drawing weight of the bow (as described in the chapter on How to Make Matched Arrows), this method can only be used as a guide and not as an absolute rule, for two bows of identical drawing weight may not necessarily have identical casts, and hence, the faster bow will require a stiffer-spined arrow than the slower bow. Therefore, if you find that your arrows are grouping to the left, going to a weaker-spined arrow may solve your problem, while on the other hand, if they are grouping to the right, a stiffer spine may be the answer.

Another factor that will affect the flight of your arrow and alter your spine requirements is the degree to which the arrow rest on the bow handle is set away from dead center. The farther away from center this rest is, the more handle the arrow must bend around in flight, and hence the weaker its spine should be to allow for this flexing. The closer to dead center this rest is brought, the closer the arrow is brought into the line of aim, and the less handle it has to curve around, with a consequent reduction in basic spine requirement. A dead center position, however, has been found unsuitable, since even with no handle for the arrow to buckle around, the fact that the string is not released in a straight line but actually rolls around the finger tips when let go, and the fact that an arrow shaft will buckle somewhat from the sudden acceleration, even when it has no handle pressure against its side, will cause it to follow an erratic course regardless of the fact that it is being pushed straight along its line of aim.

Center-shot bows have arrow rests that are about ⅛ inch to left of center, which is about the right amount to compensate for the release action and arrow flight characteristics. Bows of this type are favored by tournament archers because, putting less lateral stress on an arrow shaft, they can shoot arrows of much lighter spine and weight without fear of breakage from bending at the bow handle. The advantage of this is a faster, flatter trajectory, the arrow following the path of aim with a minimum of oscillation to affect its velocity.

While the arrow tends to oscillate from side to side upon release, it should not be allowed to oscillate vertically, as this would make the arrow sloppy in flight. An arrow will oscillate vertically if it is nocked too low on the string, and hence forced to ride up and over the arrow rest. To avoid this, the nocking point on the string should be set about ⅛ inch above the line extending 90 degrees from string to arrow rest.

The feathers on an arrow act as spiral wind vanes, causing the arrow to spin and straighten out on its flight course. They also contribute a considerable amount of drag and should not be any larger than necessary to perform their function. The small target points on a target arrow cut through the air with practically no resistance and therefore these arrows can get by with a minimum of fletching.

On a hunting arrow, the broadhead with its flat spinning surface tends to act as a wind vane in front of the arrow, causing it to windplane in flight, and this must be counteracted by using large feathers.

Much scientific research and experimentation is constantly being done to determine the best designs and materials for archery equipment, and as each year goes by, new improvements developed in the laboratory and proven in the field are made available to the archer. By knowing something of the workings of the bow and arrow, the archer in turn will be better equipped to choose the type of equipment that best fits his needs. •

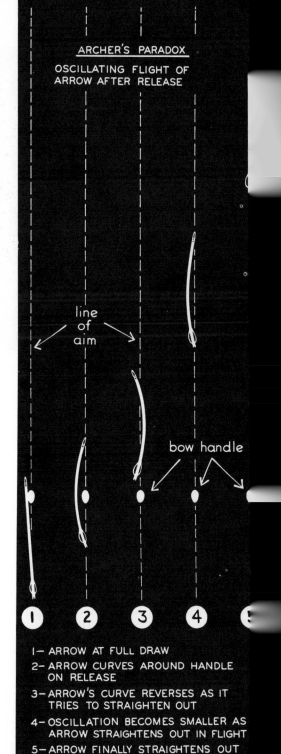

ARCHER'S PARADOX

OSCILLATING FLIGHT OF ARROW AFTER RELEASE

line of aim

bow handle

1 2 3 4

1— ARROW AT FULL DRAW

2— ARROW CURVES AROUND HANDLE ON RELEASE

3— ARROW'S CURVE REVERSES AS IT TRIES TO STRAIGHTEN OUT

4— OSCILLATION BECOMES SMALLER AS ARROW STRAIGHTENS OUT IN FLIGHT

5— ARROW FINALLY STRAIGHTENS OUT AND FOLLOWS LINE OF FLIGHT

Choice of Equipment

Learn to shoot with a light bow first, then you can move on to a heavier bow without the handicap of trying to learn how to shoot a bow with undeveloped muscles.

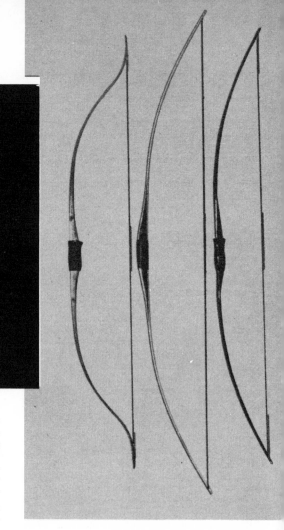

Low-priced beginners' bows: Stemmler Fiberglas recurve, 54", 30-50 lbs., price: $15; Gelco 900 laminated bow, 60", 26-60 lbs., price: $20; Paul Bunyan 400 Jr. Scout, straight-end solid Fiberglas bow, 54", available in 20 or 27 lbs., price: $9.95.

A S WITH any hobby or sport, the beginner in archery is faced with the problem of choosing the type of equipment that will best fit his individual needs. Talking to other archers can be more hindrance than help, for what has proven satisfactory for one archer may be entirely wrong for another. Unfortunately, it is all too common for a neophyte to acquire his enthusiasm for archery from hearing or reading of the exploits of some expert archer and then setting out to emulate him by buying the type of equipment he recommends, not realizing that he is probably not ready for such advanced equipment. The expert has been shooting for years and has developed the muscle power needed for handling his advanced tackle, but the beginner who prides himself on his strength will soon find that there are some muscles even he hasn't gotten around to developing. The mere fact that you can take a 50-lb. bow off the rack and draw it to 28 inches with apparent ease doesn't mean that you can do it all day long —and that's the test you must pass if you want a 50-lb. bow.

Before buying any equipment, however, you should decide in what field of archery you're most interested. As a rule, most archers look forward to hunting and hence gravitate toward the type of equipment and

shooting practice that will best fit them for this field of activity. However, there are those who have no interest in hunting and plan only to shoot at targets, or compete in tournaments, and they should get the type of equipment most suited to such purposes. The archer who wants both to hunt and do target work can get equipment that will serve him well in both fields.

As a rule, a good target bow will also work well as a hunting bow, though there are hunting bows which would not do as well on the target range. The main thing

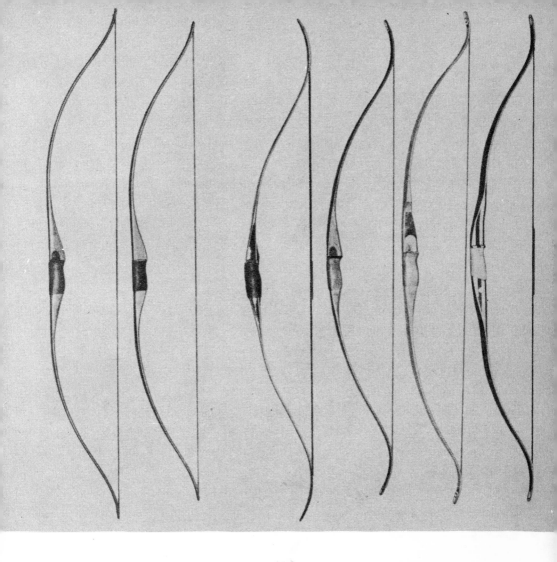

Medium-priced bows (good for both hunting and target shooting): Bear Polar, semi-recurve, 64", glass face and back, 35-75 lbs., price: $29.50; Bear Cub, semi-recurve, 62", 28" draw limit, glass face and back, 20-60 lbs., price: $22.50.

Higher-priced recurves (all laminated bows with glass face and back): Gelco 800, 60", 25-75 lbs., price: $43; Bear Kodiak, 60", 35-75 lbs., price: $50; Bear Kodiak Special, 64", 35-75 lbs., price: $59.50; Smithwick, 66", 25-100 lbs., price: $60.

for the beginner, however, is to get a bow that he can shoot repeatedly without strain. Forget the fact that you can lift a 150-lb. bar bell over your head and tear a fat telephone directory in half with your bare hands. That 50-lb. bow that seems so easy to pull the first few times will seem like a thousand pounds by the time you've pulled it a dozen or more times, and your hands will be shaking so, you'll have difficulty hitting the bale, let alone the target. If this happens after shooting just 12 arrows, think how you'll feel after shooting 144 arrows,

which is required on some competitive target courses. The answer is, you'll never get that far. You'll have discarded your heavy bow in disgust and decided that archery is not for you—"there must be a trick to it!"

But there's no trick to it—just simple common sense. You pick a light inexpensive bow to begin with—say a 25- or 30-pounder—and practice with it until you get good. It won't be hard, because you won't be under the severe strain of a heavy bow. You'll be able to hold steady and perfect

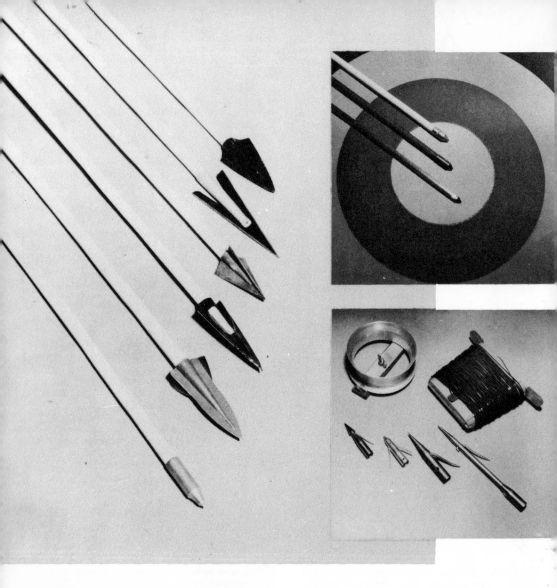

your aim, and without realizing it, you'll be developing the dormant muscles needed to pull the heavier bows. After a few months of practice, the light bow will feel like a toy and you'll be ready for your regular, heavier bow. Your shooting technique will have been perfected and you'll move on to the heavier bow without the handicap of trying to learn how to shoot a bow with undeveloped muscles.

There are a number of good, low-priced bows on the market, ranging in price from $10.00 to $20.00, which are ideal for the beginner. In this range there are some excellent solid Fiberglas bows which will take a lot of abuse and serve well for developing skill and form. Although some of these low-priced bows come in weights up to 65 lbs.,

they do not have the cast of the more expensive laminated bows and therefore are not as good for hunting. The best way to find out what weight bow to start with is to try out a few bows. Almost every good archery shop has a small range where you can shoot at a target. Take the bow of your choice and shoot about 36 arrows. If your shoulders aren't sore and your last arrows group as well as your first, the bow is not too heavy for you. Actually, you should be able to hold a bow steady at full draw for at least six seconds. If you can't, you're over-bowed.

When you're ready for your regular bow, you'll have many good designs and makes from which to choose. Among the best values in the medium-priced range are the

Far left, hunting broadheads, from top to bottom: two-blade, Howard Hill-type, three-blade, four-blade, six-blade broadhead and field point.

Top left, target arrows with target points: top arrow, wood; middle, Fiberglas; bottom, aluminum.

Left, bow reels and fishing points: RotaBarb round reel, Bear flat reel; Black Diamond and Hill's Hornet points for smaller fish; two larger heads are RotaBarb points for big game fish.

Above, Bear Razor Head, with razor insert being added to two-blade broadhead to convert it to a four-blade. Alongside is modified three-blade broadhead with hooks filed into rear of blades.

Bear Polar and the Bear Cub bows (shown in photos). These will serve both for hunting and target work. In the more expensive range are the Smithwick custom bows, the Joe Fries custom bow, the Bear Kodiak Special and other similar designs which are stable target bows and also good for hunting.

The 60-inch Bear Kodiak and the 60-inch Gelco 800 bow (shown in photo) are better suited to hunting than to target work because of their shorter length and the fact that they are lighter and faster bows. A hunting bow can be heavier than a target bow, since it isn't used as often and therefore does not put as much strain on the archer. A bow hunter may go all day and shoot as few as three arrows while the target archer shoots arrows all day—and his last one has to be as accurate as his first. Some hunters keep a heavy, 55 to 65-lb. bow for hunting only and do their target shooting with a lighter, 45 to 48-lb. bow. This is okay if you can afford it, but if you can't, you'll have to make your lighter target bow do for the hunting, not the heavier hunting bow do for the target rounds.

The next item on the list of requirements is the arrow. In this department you'll find target arrows, hunting arrows, fishing arrows, field arrows, wooden arrows, aluminum arrows, Fiberglas arrows, practice arrows and matched arrows. Arrows might easily prove to be the most expensive part of your equipment for they take the most abuse and get lost frequently. Actually, the arrow is your most important piece of equipment. It is the missile that must find its mark and will only fly true if it is well balanced, perfectly straight, and matched in spine to your bow weight. It is a fact that a good bow cannot make a bad arrow fly well, while a good arrow will fly well even when shot from a poor bow.

Practice arrows are generally cheap, unmatched arrows sold at a bargain rate because they do not have the quality to fit in with matched groups. Such arrows are good for practice and for youngsters to shoot with, but for serious precision shooting, they're worthless. For good shooting, you should have matched arrows: arrows that have been graded according to spine, weight, and straightness, and matched to your particular bow weight and cast. These come in sets and are somewhat more expensive than the unmatched variety.

Arrows come in three basic materials: wood, aluminum and Fiberglas. The latter two are more durable and more expensive, but in the long run you save money by not breaking as many as you would when shooting wooden arrows. Aluminum arrows will bend, but unless they buckle, they can usually be straightened out again. Fiberglas arrows, such as the Duro Glass type, are the most rugged of the three. They won't bend, but may sometimes rupture from being hit by another arrow or from striking some hard object a glancing blow.

Aluminum and glass arrows are excellent for target shooting because of their machine-precision uniformity in spine, weight and stiffness. They are generally considered too expensive for hunting arrows; there, wood is the favored material, for economical reasons.

Target arrows have small target points and small feathers. Field arrows have larger field points, which generally match the broadhead points in weight, and are used as substitutes for broadheads when practicing in the field. The theory is that with a point that weighs the same as a broadhead, you can get in some broadhead practice without risking your more expensive broadheads. However, it doesn't quite work out that way, because an arrow with a field point doesn't fly exactly like an arrow with a broadhead, the broadhead having a larger planing surface which gives the arrow different flying characteristics. So, if you want to get good with a broadhead for hunting purposes, practice with a cheap broadhead, shooting it into soft targets that will not damage or dull the blade too much.

For hunting, you will need a good broadhead, and if you ask 10 bow hunters which is the best broadhead, you will probably get 10 different answers. Every hunter has his own pet theories as to what qualities a good broadhead should have. Some favor the two-blade broadhead, some the three-blade, and still others the four and six-blade. Howard Hill, working to combat the planing effect of the broadhead, designed a two-blade broadhead with open sides and concave edges which he swears by. Hugh Rich, who has downed many a deer, favors the three and four-blade broadheads, feeling that a broad open wound is better than a deep narrow one. According to his experience, the two-blade broadhead penetrates deeper, but leaves such a narrow slit opening in the skin that often this slit closes and the deer is lost because there is no blood trail to follow. The three and four-

Blunts for small game include, left to right: rubber blunts in two sizes, cartridge shell with nail driven through it and curved, blunt tips, cartridge shells for improvised blunts, cut-down broadheads.

blade broadheads, however, open a flap in the skin and, though the penetration may not be as deep, the cross-flap opening in the hide is more likely to stay open and let the blood flow out. And the blood trail is the most important factor in recovering wounded game.

The latest gimmick in broadheads currently proving itself in the field is the hooked, three-blade Bodkin. Three sharp, forward-pointing hooks are filed into the trailing edges of the blades of an ordinary three-blade broadhead. These sharp hooks serve to hook into and sever any tough veins which might slide past the broadhead blade without getting cut open. Another popular hunting point is the Bear four-blade Razorhead, a combination two- or four-blade broadhead that has a replace-able, razor-sharp insert to convert it from a two-blade to a four-blade broadhead.

For small game such as rabbits, squirrels, birds, etc., blunt points are used instead of sharpened broadheads. Blunts kill by shock instead of by penetration, and small game generally takes a lot more killing than does big game. A rabbit run through with a broadhead can disappear from sight, arrow and all, leaving no trail to follow, while a blunt will bowl it over right on the spot.

As shown, ordinary cartridge shells can be fitted over arrow shafts and used as blunts. These can be improved further by driving a nail through the side of the shell casing and arrow shaft, cutting the protruding ends off to a projecting length of about ½ inch on either side, and bending these forward in an arc (as shown in photo). This tends to increase the shocking power and makes the blunt more deadly. Blunts are also made of rubber, and from broadheads with their points cut down.

Shooting birds on the wing can cost you a lot of arrows, if you miss. For an arrow shot into the air can, as the old poet wrote, "fall to earth you know not where." To avoid this, you can use floo-floos—arrows which are strictly for the birds. These have spiral fletching which creates a drag and prevents the arrow from flying too far. Up to about 25 yards, however, the floo-floo is quite accurate, but not as fast as a conventionally fletched arrow, so you'd better catch your birds napping if you want them to stick around for the kill.

For fishing, you will want heavy arrows with special fishing points, and, for the smaller fish, a bow reel that tapes to the back of the bow and holds the line attached to the arrow. The fishing head is a point with a hinged barb that opens up after entering the fish and keeps it from getting away. Since you are shooting down into the water at close range, you have no trajectory to deal with and your arrow need not be fletched. Wooden shafts will give the arrow too much buoyancy and reduce its penetration into the water, making it unsuited for deeper fish. Bob Markworth uses glass arrows filled with water to get fish that are below the surface.

Although there are several ways used to determine your correct arrow length, the beginner should get an arrow slightly longer than these calculations show. This is because he has not yet developed his form to a point where his draw length will be the same each time, and if he picks an arrow length that is on the borderline, he will run the risk of over-drawing an arrow and shooting it through his hand. •

Spirally fletched floo-floos are used for bird hunting, have effective range of about 25 yards.

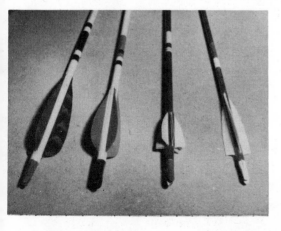

Fletching varies according to purpose: hunting arrows have large feathers, target arrows, small.

How to String the Bow

Failure to observe a few simple precautions when stringing your bow could result in serious injury.

STRANGE as it may seem, stringing (or bracing) a bow is one of the most dangerous phases of archery. Archers have lost eyes, teeth, and consciousness simply by failing to observe a few simple safeguards when stringing their bows. Such mishaps are more common with the recurve bows than with the straight-end longbows, but either type is capable of giving you a nasty wallop if you fail to string it properly.

To string a bow, first set the lower bow tip in under the arch of your right foot, resting it on the welt of your shoe and not on the ground. Setting the bow tip on the ground and then stepping on it will fray the string and damage the bow tip. Make sure the bowstring is properly nocked on this lower tip. Some archers play it safe by keeping a rubber band wrapped around the nocked loop at this end to eliminate the chance of its coming loose.

Now, with the lower tip properly nocked and set against the arch of your foot, and the back of the bow facing you, grasp the handle of the bow with your right hand. Using the thumb and forefinger of your left hand, encircle the upper limb and slide the free loop of the bowstring upward

At left, Jo McCubbins strings her bow by flexing it over her right knee. This gives her sufficient leverage without putting any twisting strain on the recurve tips. Below, Bob Hylton braces bow against foot, flexes bow and pushes top loop up to nock.

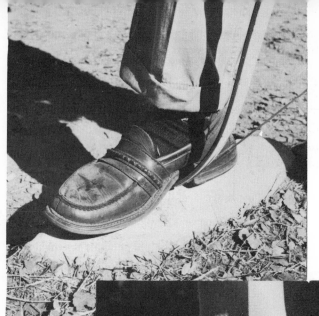

To string a bow, first set the lower bow tip in under the arch of your right foot, resting it on the welt of your shoe and not on the ground. Setting the bow on the ground, as shown at left, and then stepping on it, will fray and weaken the loop, possibly damage the bow tip as well. Make sure the bowstring is properly nocked on this lower tip.

toward the string groove. Make sure thumb and forefinger wrap around the bow limb, so there won't be any chance of the limb slipping out of your grasp. Don't get your finger under the loop either, unless you can afford to lose a fingernail—and are willing to suffer the pain of losing it.

To slide the string loop up to the nock, you will have to flex the bow. This is done by holding back on the handle section with the right hand and pushing forward with the left hand as you slide the string up the limb. The right hand should only hold the bow, not pull backward on it to bend it. The bending is done by the forward pressure applied to the upper limb with the left hand as it flexes the bow and simultaneously moves the string up to the nock. The string should be stretched taut at all times while it is being pushed up to the nock. This will keep the lower loop from becoming un-nocked, as might happen if the bow were flexed enough to let the string hang loose.

When you feel the upper loop slip into the string groove, don't relax. This is the real danger point, for if the string is improperly nocked and you release your grip, the tension of the flexed bow can un-nock the string and the limb will then snap back toward your face with terrific force. To avoid this, develop the habit of turning the bow 90 degrees by swinging the handle in toward you, letting the bow pivot on its bottom tip while still maintaining the same grip and pressure used to flex the bow for nocking. As soon as the bow is turned with its back away from your face, you can relax your grip with the left hand and lift the bow with your right hand to inspect the nocks. Hold the bow well away from your face when inspecting it, not up close to it. If a weak string should break at this point, it could lash your face.

To protect his face against the possibility of the recurve whipping back while stringing the bow, Bob Bennett pulls his left shoulder in to cover his face while he flexes the bow limb, as shown in photos. If the bow should slip, his shoulder would deflect the limb from his face.

To unstring a bow, follow the same procedure as above, only in reverse, this time applying pressure to the upper limb to flex it enough so that you can slip the upper loop out of its nock. Here, too, you must guard against letting the limb slip from your grasp. The best way to do this is to wrap your thumb around one side of the limb and use your forefinger to roll the

string loop out of its nock. Never use your thumb for this operation as this will weaken your grip on the bow tip and increase the chances of its slipping from your grip. Once the loop is un-nocked, let the bow straighten out gradually by relaxing the tension simultaneously with both hands.

A less strenuous method of stringing a recurve bow, favored by women archers especially, is to step in between the string and the bow with the right leg, hook the lower recurve tip around the ankle of the

Left hand flexes bow and simultaneously moves upper loop of taut bowstring up to string groove.

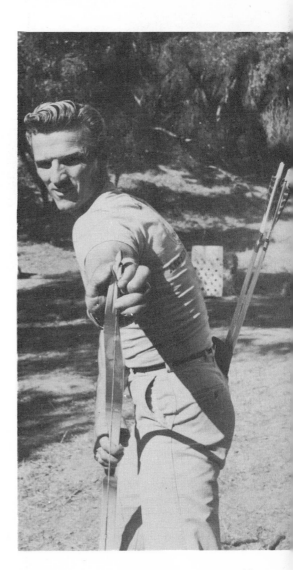

Left, wrong way to inspect nock after stringing. Holding bow tip too close to face can mean nasty whipping should string give way at this point.

Below, right way to inspect nock after stringing. Lift bow with right hand and hold bow well away from face when inspecting nocked bowstring loops.

left leg, and then, using the back of the right leg as a fulcrum, flex the bow around the right leg by pulling forward on the upper limb with the right hand, at the same time moving the string up with the left hand until it slips into the upper nock. While this method employs the best principles of leverage and makes it much easier to brace a bow, it is not a good method because there is always the danger of twisting the recurves out of shape and ruining the bow. This happens most often with the lower recurve, which, due to the oblique angle of the bow in relation to the archer's body, is braced unevenly around

the left ankle and gets twisted sideways if the upper limb is pulled inward toward the body when it is flexed, instead of straight forward in line with the bow's natural flexing direction.

A better way to apply leverage when bracing a recurve is to follow the same procedure as outlined for the straight-end longbow, but use your right knee for an additional brace as shown. This technique, as used by Jo McCubbins, consists of bending the bow across the right knee while its lower tip is wedged under the arch of the left foot. This allows you two hands for bending the bow, the left hand giving an

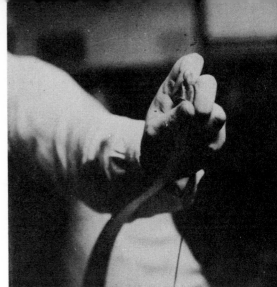

At left, Bob Bennett practices safety first when stringing bow. By throwing shoulder in front of face, head is protected should bow spring back.

Above, correct way to unstring bow. Thumb encircles bow tip; forefinger is used to unloop string from nock. Never loosen with thumb; thumb keeps bow from springing back should there be a slip.

Below, Jo McCubbins demonstrates the "step-over" method of stringing recurve bow. This method is tricky though and can cause twisted recurve tip.

assist while the right hand does most of the work. Your knee, of course, should be under the heavy center section of the bow and not under any part of the flexing limb, as this would cause the lower limb to be flexed more than the upper limb, thus creating uneven stresses on the bow. Once the string is nocked by this method, maintain your grip on the bow but move your knee away. Then swing the handle away from your body to pivot the bow around to a position where its face will be toward you, You can then relax your grip without fear of the recurve snapping back at you should it be improperly nocked. •

Target Shooting Technique

Choose the style of shooting most suited to your field of archery—then stick with it until perfection is achieved.

NATURALLY, the aim of every archery enthusiast is to shoot a bow with great accuracy, placing arrow after arrow in the gold. How close he comes to this goal will depend on his coordination, shooting technique, judgment—and plenty of practice. Only with months of serious practice can the archer's qualities be perfected to that point which separates the everyday archer from the skilled marksman.

Before you begin your practice, however, you should know something about correct technique, for, without it, you're just sailing arrows through space to little effect. In the old days, there was no set standard of drawing and releasing. Archers were pulling back in the air somewhere near the ear. The arrow was way off to one side. The head was seldom in the same position. And results were equally inconsistent. Then, some 15 or 18 years ago, Russ Hoogerhyde decided to do something about this and settled on a technique of anchoring beneath the chin with the bowstring bisecting the chin and nose. With this technique, Hoogerhyde smashed all archery records. His system is still the predominant one used by target archers.

All this points up the fact that if you can eliminate the human element in archery and convert yourself as nearly as possible to a machine, you're bound to become a good archer. It is the human element that we have most to contend with in archery and the way to overcome it is to train ourselves to operate with machine-like precision, doing everything right in exactly the same manner every time, not just now and then.

Just what is ideal in archery can be debated as long as individuality exists among archers. Many experts say that for target archery the Hoogerhyde under-the-chin anchor is a must, but then along comes a guy named Joe Fries, using nothing but a corner-of-the-mouth anchor, who knocks the whole argument into a cocked hat by copping the National Target Archery Championship two years in a row, 1955 and 1956. Then, too, you hear that the *only* way is to select one technique, either the

Far left, National Instinctive Champions Leslie Speaks and Jo McCubbins take aim on archery range. Bow should be held in loose grip, as demonstrated by Ken Cooper in photo above left. Heeling the bow in a tight fist grip, above right, is wrong.

chin anchor or the cheek anchor, and stick to it. But what about Ken Cooper, archery instructor and Recreation Director for the Los Angeles Department of Recreation and Parks, who uses both techniques interchangeably and very successfully? The fact is, whatever technique you find most comfortable and effective is the technique you should use, and if you can handle two techniques with equal efficiency, then you've got an advantage because each technique will complement the other and broaden your scope as an archer.

Before you can make your choice, however, you will have to learn the fundamentals of shooting. It's just as easy to learn

the right way as it is to learn the wrong way, and bad habits undeveloped will not have to be unlearned. Basically, the procedure for shooting consists of taking a stance, nocking, drawing, holding and releasing. Each is equally important to good shooting and should be given full concentration. Since the beginner must practice with standing targets before he becomes proficient enough to hunt with bow and arrow, the following instructions are for target archery, where conditions are more stabilized and conducive to the development of good shooting form. Once the archer has developed good form and can shoot a consistently good score, he is ready

24

RIGHT: at full draw, arm is extended straight out toward the target with shoulder held in line.

WRONG: pulling shoulder in under chin to rest muscles brings arm into painful path of string.

Starting draw, bowstring is hooked inside first joints of three fingers. Thumb is turned down.

Drawing, fingers open up to let string roll forward. Only finger tips hold string at full draw.

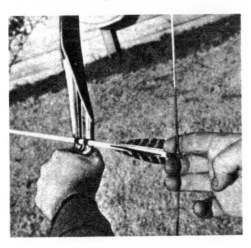

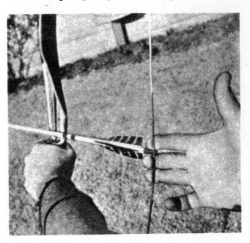

to move into the more advanced phases of archery, such as roving ranges and bow hunting, which call for the development of good judgment of distance and performance under a variety of conditions. First, however, the following should be practiced and learned:

STANCE: The first requirement for standardizing your shooting technique is to stand correctly. Your weight should be distributed equally on both feet, with body straight and erect. Stand at right angles to the target, your left shoulder facing it, feet well apart and set firmly on an imaginary line leading to the target. Hold your bow in a loose grip with your left hand, bow limbs horizontal to the ground, string up and arm hanging down in relaxed position. If your stance is right, your body will be well balanced on a firm footing and less likely to lean or sway when you shoot.

NOCKING: Nocking consists of fitting an arrow to the bowstring. Though this may seem like a simple operation, it is, nevertheless, a very critical one. The arrow must be nocked at the identical point on the string each time. A difference of as little as ⅛ inch above or below this point will be multiplied in direct ratio to the distance to the target, putting the arrow off your target as much as 16 inches at 50 yards— enough to miss a deer completely.

The best way to make sure of nocking your arrow at the same point each time is to make a "nocking point" on your string to act as a back-stop against which your arrow nock can be held. The nocking point is usually a ball of serving thread, wrapped around the string at the point where the arrow is to be nocked and covered with beeswax. This point should be located on the string where it will hold the arrow at right angles to the string with the front end of the arrow resting on the arrow plate of the bow handle. Your nocking point can be located either above the arrow or below it—or you can make two points, one above and one below, to hold the arrow nock snugly between them. The latter method is suitable for field and target archery where you can take your time nocking, but for hunting, where you have to nock fast to get a second shot at your quarry, it is impractical. Some hunters prefer to put the

nocking point above the arrow; if the nocked arrow catches in shrubbery while stalking, its nock will hold against the nocking point and keep the arrow from sliding up along the string and becoming un-nocked. Howard Hill, however, prefers his nocking point below the arrow; he finds it easier to nock his arrow high on the string and slide it down to the nocking point when in a hurry than to nock it low and slide it up to the nocking point. Whether you set your nocking point above or below the arrow is a matter of personal choice and is immaterial marksmanshipwise, as long as it lines up the arrow correctly.

The arrow plate, or rest, on the bow handle, is another important point in lining up the arrow. There was a time when the top of the bow hand was used as the arrow rest, but because the bow wasn't always gripped in exactly the same spot, this system wasn't very satisfactory. Just as

Recreation Director Ken Cooper demonstrates high cheek anchor, best suited for short-range targets.

Ken shifts arrow to target archer's under-chin low anchor. Note difference in angles of shaft.

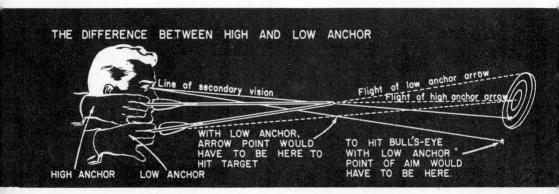

THE DIFFERENCE BETWEEN HIGH AND LOW ANCHOR

Line of secondary vision

Flight of low anchor arrow
Flight of high anchor arrow

WITH LOW ANCHOR, ARROW POINT WOULD HAVE TO BE HERE TO HIT TARGET

TO HIT BULL'S-EYE WITH LOW ANCHOR POINT OF AIM WOULD HAVE TO BE HERE.

HIGH ANCHOR   LOW ANCHOR

⅛-inch variance up and down the bow-string will throw an arrow off target by 16 inches at 50 yards, so, too, will a ⅛-inch variance high or low in gripping the bow handle. The answer to this problem is the arrow rest, which has become standard with all good bows.

With your nocking point and arrow rest taking the guesswork out of lining up the arrow, the only thing left to do when nocking an arrow is to make sure the cock feather, which is the one mounted at right angles to the nock, is positioned on the left side of the string. To nock the arrow, hold the bow away from your body in a more or less horizontal position to the ground with the string held back toward your ribs. Place the arrow on the arrow rest and hold it there lightly by looping the forefinger of your left hand over it. Then, move your right hand under the bowstring, grip the arrow nock between your first two fingers,

When shooting with the bow tilted, the head must be tilted, too, to keep everything properly in line.

making sure that the cock feather is up, and with these fingers, draw the arrow back until its nock engages the bowstring. Then slide it over to the nocking point, raise your bow up to vertical shooting position, remove your left forefinger from around the arrow and you are ready to draw.

Another method of nocking is to rest the arrow across the bow and string, then take the arrow nock between your thumb and forefinger and spin it until the cock feather is up and at right angles to the string. Now slide the arrow forward off the string, then back onto it with the nock fitting snugly over the string. Slide it over to the nocking point, hook your three drawing fingers around the string, and you are ready to draw.

DRAWING: Hold the bow with your left hand in a loose, relaxed grip. Don't clutch it in a death grip as this will cause every movement to be telegraphed to the bow and result in poor scoring. The less hand you place on the bow handle, the less shock wave your arm will absorb and consequently there will be less chance of a jolt to spoil your aim. Some championship archers hold the bow so loosely that it jumps forward in their hands on release.

To practice the right grip, spread the fingers of your left hand and fit the bow handle into the crotch between your thumb and forefinger. You will notice that, even with your fingers spread, you can draw the bow and it will stay fast against the heel of your thumb. Your hand should be held at an oblique angle, elbow pointed out and not down to bring the arm and wrist out of the path of the bowstring. Now bring your fingers lightly around the bow handle, cradling it in a loose, relaxed grip, to keep it from jumping completely out of your hand on release. This type of loose grip will not interfere with the free action of the bow and will let the arrow take a natural

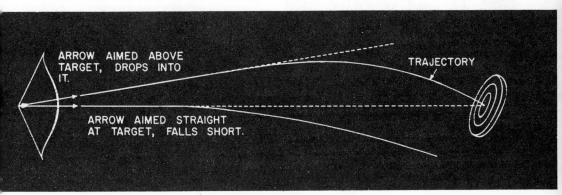

ARROW AIMED ABOVE TARGET, DROPS INTO IT.

TRAJECTORY

ARROW AIMED STRAIGHT AT TARGET, FALLS SHORT.

path to the target on release. To some degree, it will also help compensate for the sensitivity of a recurve, for, if you flinch and pull slightly to the right or left with the string on release, the bow, held in a loose grip, will tend to pivot in your hand and line up with the direction of your draw. Of course, you shouldn't flinch, but there are occasions during a hunt when it can't be helped.

To draw, raise your bow to vertical posi-

tion, left arm extended straight out toward the target, and draw straight back with your right arm, using the muscles of your back and shoulders rather than your arm to do the work. At full draw, your right elbow should be in a straight line with the arrow. It should point neither up nor down. Beware of the tendency to ease the effort by moving your head forward to meet the string. This practice will result in a short draw and sufficient loss of power to upset your aim.

As you draw, take a deep breath and tilt your head slightly to bring your right eye directly over the shaft of the arrow when it reaches its anchor point. Your anchor point can be either on your cheek at the corner of your mouth, or it can be under your chin with the string bisecting your chin and nose. These methods will be discussed more fully later in the chapter.

The finger grip on your string as you draw back is another important operation that must be done right. Your nocked arrow is lightly wedged between the forefinger and middle finger of your left hand. One other finger, the ring finger, is used with these two to hold the string. These three fingers are hooked around the string at the start of the draw, with the string cutting into the first joint of all three and the thumb turned down. As you draw back, let the fingers open slightly and allow the string to roll forward until it is held only by the finger tips just forward of the first joints. This unrolling action of the fingers will also serve to hold the arrow under tension against the bow and permit you to remove the left forefinger that was curled around the arrow and return it to its position with the other fingers on the bow handle. All three fingers should pull equally on the string while drawing.

HOLDING: If you are not over-bowed, you should be able to hold your stance at full draw for a few seconds, time enough to check yourself for mistakes and aim the arrow. If all is well, at full draw your left arm will be extended straight out toward the target, your right elbow straight back, with elbow, arrow, and left arm forming a straight line toward the target. Your bow will be held in a loose grip, your left arm turned elbow out and locked at the joint leaving a clear path for the string when released. If the string hits your forearm on release, you haven't been holding right.

Your feet are firmly planted on the ground about 10 to 15 inches apart and at right angles to the target, body erect and chest out. Your head is cocked at a comfortable angle to bring your right eye directly over the arrow. Your right hand, with thumb down, is anchored against your cheek or chin, and the pile of the arrow is resting on the arrow plate of the bow.

This is the stance you must duplicate exactly each time you shoot an arrow. If you've done everything right and sent an arrow straight into the gold, you can only repeat that performance if you do everything again *in exactly the same manner*. That is the secret of good shooting: consistency—doing everything the same way each time. Then, if your aim is good and your arrows matched, you'll hit the bull's-eye every time.

RELEASING: When you've drawn, anchored and aimed to your satisfaction, all that is left to do is release. Your release should be smooth and relaxed, letting the taut string do the work and not your fingers. At full draw, your fingers should be straight, except for the first joints which are slightly crooked around the bowstring. The tension of the bowstring will be trying to open them up, a force which you should cooperate with, not fight, when you decide to release. To release, simply relax your fingers and allow the string to get away under its own power. Don't jerk back or "pluck" on the string when you release, as this will pull it out of line and deflect the arrow from its true course. If you relax properly during the release, your right hand will never leave your cheek but only move back a few inches and hold while the arrow hits its mark. If your hand springs out in space behind or away from your cheek, you've flubbed your release.

"Creeping" is another way of flubbing a release. It consists of moving your fingers forward slightly during the release, thus letting your arrow creep forward a little before it is released. Creeping usually results from fatigue or an effort to relieve some of the tension on the fingers by letting up slightly on the string. This is disastrous to good marksmanship because it reduces the power behind the arrow, causing it to fall short of its mark. Remember

that the weight of your bow, and hence its hurling power, is calculated to the full length of your draw, and if that draw is 28 inches, it should be drawn to its full 28 inches each time. An arrow that is allowed to creep up as little as one-half inch will reduce the weight of the bow by a pound or more and thereby throw everything out of balance.

After releasing, hold your release stance until the arrow has found its mark. This is called the "follow through" and is important to the development of good shooting form.

ANCHORING: Hand in hand with the mechanics of shooting a bow go the mechanics of aiming, which begin with the anchor point. Unlike a rifle bullet, which has an almost flat trajectory, the arrow leaving a bow follows a definitely curved path, which factor must be carefully taken into account when aiming at a target. The farther the target is from the archer, the higher he will have to shoot his arrow in order for it to

Above, correct release: relax fingers and allow string to get away smoothly. Plucking the string, below, will deflect arrow from intended course.

reach its mark. This is where the problem of aiming is most acute, for while the archer can get his eye directly over the arrow and see that it is aimed straight at the target and not to the right or left of it, there is no such simple method of accurately estimating by eye the amount of elevation required to reach a target where the distance is unknown. That can only come with long hours of practice and a full knowledge of how your bow works.

Since it is impractical to bring the arrow up directly under the eye and sight down its shaft the way you sight along a gun barrel (this would force you into an uncomfortable and awkward stance and, because of the trajectory, you'd never see the target, you'd be aiming so high above it) new methods of aiming had to be developed and standardized to meet the specific problems of archery. Today, the two most popular and pretty nearly standard anchors for aiming are the chin, or low anchor, and the cheek, or high anchor.

The main purpose of the anchor is to establish a fixed point under your sighting eye to which you can draw and hold consistently. Without such a fixed point, the length of your draw and tilt of your arrow would vary enough between shots to throw you off your target. With the cheek anchor, which is actually a corner-of-the-mouth anchor, you draw back until one of the three fingers holding the string is firmly planted against the corner of the mouth. Most popularly, the forefinger is the one anchored at the mouth corner. Either of the other two fingers will raise the butt end of the arrow enough to change its course of flight and may prove awkward to hold. Although you're anchoring at the corner of your mouth, your anchor finger should be braced against tooth or bone and not just the fleshy part of the face. This will give you a more stable anchor point, whereas flesh alone, because of its stretching qualities, provides a poor anchor. The thumb should be turned down and hooked under the jaw when at full draw.

The high anchor is best suited for short-range targets and therefore it is predominantly used by hunters and field archers. It brings the butt of the arrow up closer to the sighting eye, thus giving you a tighter aiming picture, as shown in diagram.

The low or under-the-chin anchor is preferred by most target archers who shoot at more distant targets and use sights on their bows. With this anchor, you draw the arrow back directly under your chin, letting the string cut across your chin, lips and nose as shown in photos. This is a more

accurate way of shooting because it gives you three check points—your chin, lips, and nose—to make sure you're drawing to the exact anchor point each time. Some archers play it even safer by putting a little button or ball of serving on the string at a point above the arrow nock where it will come in contact with their lips. This "kisser" then serves as a further check point to keep them from anchoring too low under the chin. If this button doesn't kiss the lips just right with each draw, then something has been changed in the draw. With this draw, too, the thumb must be turned down. A thumb poking up in the air with either draw indicates tension, and tension will not help anyone's archery. It also gets in the way and makes for poor anchoring. How each of these two anchoring methods affects the aiming technique will be seen when we study the optics of aiming.

AIMING: There are three distinct methods of aiming: the sight method, the point-of-aim method, and the instinctive. The first method utilizes a mechanical guide in the form of a pin sight on the bow which, when properly adjusted and set on target while aiming, will direct the arrow to the bull's-eye. With the second method, no sight is

Bill Moran, Arizona State Field Archery Champion, demonstrates his preferred under-the-chin anchor. Note how the bowstring bisects chin, lips and nose. In release and follow-through, Bill's relaxed hand does not leave his cheek until after arrow hits its mark.

used. Instead the archer aims by means of a "space picture," seeing the target by direct vision and the point of the arrow by indirect vision. With his eye still focused on the target, he puts the point of his arrow on a spot some distance below it, depending on how far away the target is, and shoots. The spot he put his arrow on is called the "point of aim," and if his arrow hits the bull's-eye, he knows he's picked the right point of aim and can duplicate the shot by setting his next arrow on the same point of aim. The space picture or point-of-aim method of aiming is often erroneously called the instinctive method of shooting, but that's not the way archery instructor Bob Bennett of Pro Archery in Costa Mesa, California, teaches instinctive shooting. The way he teaches it, the instinctive shooter uses no sight or space picture aiming aids. He focuses his eyes on the bull's-eye and sees nothing else. Purely by instinct, he draws and fires. The theory is that the natural instincts of man are more reliable than his powers of mechanical judgment. Just as a person can train himself to throw a ball or shoot a slingshot with accuracy, both of which actions are performed by instinct, so, too, can he train himself to shoot a bow instinctively with-

out resorting to such mechanical aids as sights and space pictures. Thus, the true instinctive shooter aims by feel rather than by calculation. He does not concern himself with trying to estimate distances in yards or feet any more than the baseball outfielder does when he catches a high one and then flings it in to second base for a double play. His instincts, developed through long hours of practice, automatically take over and, without consciously realizing it, he's throwing with just the right amount of force and elevation to reach his target. This is the goal of the instinctive archer: to reach that point where aiming and shooting become automatic and accuracy is the result of subconscious direction rather than conscious calculation. The archer who achieves this becomes a much better hunter, since hunting conditions do not allow time for making calculations and instincts don't calculate.

To shoot instinctively, follow all the rules of stance, nocking, drawing, holding and loosing as outlined previously. These are the mechanical techniques which must be learned to perfection before accuracy can be achieved. Any inconsistencies in this pattern of operation will show up in your shooting. This goes for all methods of aim-

31

National Instinctive Field Archery Champion Leslie Speaks uses corner-of-the-mouth or tooth anchor.

ing, whether instinctive, point of aim, or sight.

Now, at full draw (the high anchor is best here), focus your eyes on the target and keep them there. Pay no attention to anything else you may see in your side or secondary vision. Your eyes, as you know, take in a wide angle of vision even though they are focused on one central object. For instinctive shooting, you must let nothing you see outside of your target distract or influence your concentration on the target. When you feel that your aim is right, shoot. You will be surprised at how close you'll come—maybe even hit the target. Shoot about a dozen arrows in this manner and note your grouping. If you are doing everything the same in your shooting technique, you'll find that your arrows are grouping fairly well. They may be grouping high, low, or off to one side. Keep practicing, concentrating always on doing everything with uniformity and focusing your eyes exclusively on the target. Before long, you'll notice that your groupings are getting

closer to the bull's-eye. Without realizing just how you do it, you'll be making compensations in your aim to bring your shots home. You will be developing your instincts and, as George Gobel would say, they're the best kind.

For these first practice sessions, work close, at about 10 yards. Then, when you get good at this short distance, move back to greater distances. But don't worry about what the measured distance is, just go through the same practice routine you followed at 10 yards and give your instincts a workout at the greater distances. In time, you will be able to draw and hit a target with the first shot, from any range, without first trying to calculate the distance.

Point-of-aim shooting is similar to instinctive, with the exception that you take in the point of your arrow with your secondary vision and set it on a point below the target when aiming. How far below the target this point is must depend on how far away the target is. At close range, this point may be as low as some point on the

Speaks holds the bow loosely, even at full draw.

ground, while at greater ranges, it gets closer to the target's dead center. Eventually, you reach a distance where the point of the arrow must be set right on the bull's-eye. This is called point-blank range, and if you know what distance this is for your particular bow, you'll have no problem hitting the gold on any target that is set at that particular distance. Every bow has its own point-blank range and it's a good idea to find out what it is for your bow before you go out shooting for high scores.

Actually, every bow has *two* point-blank ranges, one for the low anchor and one for the high anchor. The one for the low anchor is much farther than the one for the high anchor. To understand this better, suppose you draw to the high anchor and aim at a target that is at point-blank range. Your arrow point will then be aimed right on the bull's-eye of the target, but, if you could look at yourself from the side, you'd see that the arrow is pointed slightly upward to compensate for its trajectory in flight.

Now, without changing the position of

the arrow point (it's still aimed at the bull's-eye), move the anchor down to beneath the chin. This will bring the butt of the arrow down to a lower position in relation to the point, giving the arrow an even steeper upward angle. Its trajectory then would carry it high over the target, to some point beyond it. If you could set another target at this further distance, lined up so the arrow would hit the bull's-eye, you'd have the point-blank range for low-anchor aiming. This is the reason why most target archers, who shoot at more distant targets, prefer the low chin anchor. With the high cheek anchor when shooting at targets beyond point-blank range, your point of aim has to be above the target, and then your bow hand will block your view of the target and make aiming difficult.

When using the point-of-aim or space-picture aiming method, focus your eyes on the target, then bring your arrow up until its point is aimed just below the target. Never focus your eyes on the arrow but keep them fixed on the target only. The point of the arrow will appear as a blur in your side vision. Actually, you will see two arrow points, side by side, because each eye sees a separate image when focused on the distant target. If you change your focus to the arrow point, you will then see one arrow but two targets. For the purposes of good shooting, it's better to see two arrows and only one target, so keep your eyes on the target and form your space picture with only the left arrow image. If you're in doubt about which arrow image to aim with, close your left eye for a second and one of the images, the undesirable one, will disappear. However, don't aim with one eye closed. Your judgment of distance will fall off considerably with one eye since perspective and depth perception require the stereoscopic or binocular vision of both eyes. For this reason, all shooting is done with both eyes open, although one eye does the actual aiming.

The point of aim or spot below the target at which you aim the arrow point can only be determined by practice. If your arrows are going high, lower your point of aim, and if they are hitting too low, raise your point of aim. Eventually, with practice, you'll know just how far below the target to aim your arrow at various distances. As mentioned before, this spot gets closer to the target as the distance to the target increases. That's because you have to raise the point of the arrow more for a higher trajectory in order to reach the more distant targets.

The space picture is the over-all picture you see when aiming. Your eyes are focused on the target center but still see the arrow point below it. The space between the arrow point and the target center is the space picture. Some archers figure this space between arrow point and target in inches or feet *at the target,* while others prefer to see it as fractions of an inch *at the point of the arrow.* In other words, if you put a strip of white adhesive tape on the face of your bow and marked it off in fractions of an inch, starting upward from the arrow rest, you would be able to aim by putting your target opposite the marking that gave you the right space picture at the point of your arrow as calculated for that particular range. Without the tape, and calculating your space picture at the target, your point of aim for that particular range might be on the ground, say two feet below the target center. However, to be more instinctive about it, you might forget about inches and feet and just get used to forming a certain size space picture for each range without trying to estimate its spacing in inches or feet.

When using the high anchor at short-range targets, the space picture is more compact and easier to gauge because the arrow is brought up closer to the eye with

a consequent lowering of its trajectory. However, if you switched to the low anchor on the same target range, you'd have to bring the tip of your arrow down considerably to lower your trajectory. This would give you a point of aim somewhere on the ground between the target and yourself instead of up on the target just under the bull's-eye. Such a broad space picture could cause undue confusion, and therefore, the high anchor is more suitable for the shorter ranges.

Aiming with a sight is another popular method, and most accurate where the distance to the target is known. This method is similar to the one using a calibrated tape on the face of your bow as previously described, but with the added refinement of having a sliding pin on the bow that can be set for various distances. There are many fine commercial sights on the market that can be fitted to your bow. However, for a simple homemade sight, you can cement a strip of $\frac{1}{16}$-inch thick cork to the back of your bow, leading upward from the arrow rest for about five inches, and cover this with a strip of calibrated white adhesive tape. For the sight, use a small, ball-headed pin and stick this into the edge of the cork in line with the marking that corresponds to the distance to the target. The head of the pin should project out over the arrow rest. The calibrations on the tape are marked off in yards to correspond with the various target ranges. To mark them off accurately, you will first have to experiment with targets at various measured distances, setting the pin up and down the scale until you find the point which gives you the greatest accuracy for each particular distance. These points are then marked and numbered with the distances to which they correspond.

When aiming with a sight, you first set the sight to the calibration that conforms with the estimated distance to the target. Then draw and aim by putting the pinhead directly on the bull's-eye of the target. With this method, you don't bother about space pictures or point of aim. You just set the sight on target and shoot. If you've estimated the distances correctly and your shooting technique is unvaried, you'll hit the gold every time.

The sight can be used with either the high or low anchor. The low-anchor shooters prefer it because it extends the shooting range and still keeps the target in view. By extending the point-blank range, it allows the shooter to raise his ar-

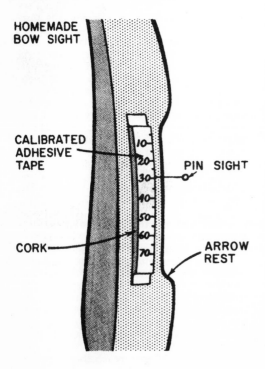

HOMEMADE BOW SIGHT

CALIBRATED ADHESIVE TAPE

PIN SIGHT

10
20
30
40
50
60
70

CORK

ARROW REST

row higher without his bow hand getting in the way of his aim, thus giving him more range within which he can use his bow sight.

These, then, are the three basic aiming methods. Each has its advantages and disadvantages. The system that will score the highest points on the target range will not necessarily bag the most game on the hunt. Since most archers take up the sport with the idea of eventually using it for hunting, they generally gravitate toward the high anchor and more or less instinctive or space picture method of aiming. The target archers who care nothing for hunting and find difficulty in estimating distances, generally prefer the low chin anchor and bow sight, which is a slower but more accurate way of shooting. For the beginner, it is best to decide in advance what field of archery he is most interested in, then choose the style of shooting most suited to that field and stick with it until perfection is achieved. But perfection will not come overnight. It takes months of practice. In the end, though, it pays off in pleasure and satisfaction for all participants. •

When aiming by means of a space picture, tilting often presents a better view of the target area.

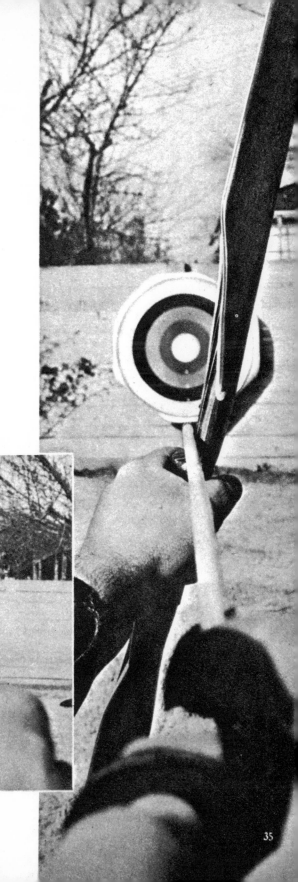

Hunting Techniques

The test of a good bow hunter is not his shooting skill, but his ability to get within close range of his quarry, a feat which gun hunters do not often have to duplicate.

HOWARD HILL, the world famous bow hunter, has probably killed more wild game with a bow and arrow than any other man alive today. His exploits with bow and arrow both on this continent and in the wilds of Africa, where he proved that he could kill an elephant with a bow and arrow, have made archery history. As an authority on the art and technique of bow hunting, Hill is tops in the field, and herewith, for the benefit of archers who would ahunting go—and what archer doesn't sooner or later get the yen to match wiles with the wild animals of the forest—are Hill's own techniques for bow hunting as told to this reporter.

"The first thing an archer should do if he plans to go in for bow hunting," says Hill, "is make sure of his equipment. He should know his bow, and especially his arrows, like a gun hunter knows his gun and the weight of his bullets."

Hill believes in using a bow as heavy in pull as he can handle without straining. If the bow is comfortable at full draw, the added weight will give the arrow a faster, flatter trajectory, which is very important in hunting. This permits the arrow to be shot from under low-hanging limbs and through foliage, whereas with a lighter bow, the arrow would have to follow a higher arc to its target and could easily be deflected by the tiniest twig. However, it's worse to be over-bowed than under-bowed, so if you have any doubts about being able to handle a heavy bow with ease and accuracy pick a lighter one that you can be sure of.

A 50-lb. bow will generally kill any animal in America and there are many ex-

At left, hunter Hill returning with jaguar shot in Yaqui River country, Mexico. Below, mountain lion treed by dogs and shot by Hill in Arizona.

Hill makes good use of his binoculars when on the hunt, steadying them on his bow tip while searching the immediate countryside for game.

Howard Hill Photos

Hill wears soft leather shoes with gum soles for stalking, stepping forward on the toe of his foot, tenderly feeling the ground before setting his weight down in order not to startle any likely game.

perienced hunters using such bows, but conditions have to be very favorable for good results. Unfortunately, the archer rarely gets the chance to shoot under conditions where he can place his arrow just where he wants it. Instead of hitting the chest cavity, an arrow may go high and hit the spine, or some thick bony plate that will stop it if it hasn't got sufficient penetration. Hill uses an 85-lb. bow for ordinary game, but since there are few archers strong enough to pull such a bow with consistent accuracy, the best advice is to try to strike a happy medium somewhere between that and the 50-lb. bow. Know the limitations of your weapon and avoid trying shots that are beyond its power.

The hunting arrow should be matched to the bow as carefully as the bow is matched to the hunter. The hunting arrow must, be efficient, accurate and tough, with the right weight, length and spine of shaft to fit the bow. The broadhead should be of the right width and the feathers of the right height and length. The broadhead which Hill uses is one which he designed after years of experimentation in the field. It has been widely copied by other manufacturers. The head consists of a V-shaped cutting edge of 18-gauge steel attached to an $\frac{11}{32}$-inch duralumin ferrule. The cutting edge, which is slightly concave, is 3⅜ inches long and flares out to a base width of 1⅛ inches. Unlike other broadheads which have broad flat surfaces to buck the wind as the arrow spins on its course, the Howard Hill broadhead uses very little metal and has no broad surfaces to catch the wind and cause the arrow to windplane. For a 50- to 65-lb. bow, Hill recommends a broadhead one inch wide by three inches in length; a ¾-inch wide by 2½-inch long blade should be used with a 35- to 40-lb. bow, and a ⅞-inch wide by

2⅝-inch long blade for a 40- to 50-lb. bow.

For small game, such as rabbits, squirrel, birds, etc., Hill uses blunts which kill by shock as well as penetration. These are .38 rifle shells fitted over $\frac{11}{32}$-inch shafts.

Before embarking on a hunt, the bow hunter should make sure his broadheads are sharp, for the sharper the cutting edge, the greater will be the arrow's penetration. In this respect, a fine saw-tooth edge will cut through tough sinew and bone better than a smooth razor edge. Hill's technique of putting a saw-tooth edge on his broadheads is to sharpen them to a razor edge first, using a small flat file. Then, turning the file on edge, he draws the corner of the file down across the sharpened blade, at the same time moving it forward along the blade from the barb end to the point. This single action of the file serves to cut a fine saw-tooth edge into the sharpened broadhead.

Hill carries a file with him on all hunting trips and sharpens his broadheads as often as they need it. This is important because, unlike a gun which kills by shock, an arrow kills by causing hemorrhage, and the sharper it is, the deeper it will penetrate.

Another important piece of equipment is the quiver. From experience, Hill has found that the best type for hunting is a medium soft leather type with an oval base which will lie flat and comfortable against the back. He favors a single shoulder strap which allows him to slide the quiver under his left arm when crawling through low brush, thus bringing the quiver into a position horizontal to the ground and preventing the arrows from catching on brush and overhead limbs. Once through the brush, he pushes the quiver back to normal position with his left hand. When reaching back for an arrow, he brings his bow hand back under the quiver and braces it while his right hand selects an arrow. Then, with one coordinated motion, his left hand comes forward with the bow and his right hand brings the arrow into nocking position.

Because an arrow doesn't have anywhere near the range of a bullet from a high-powered rifle, the bow hunter must be a better stalker than the gun hunter. He has to get very close to his game before he can get in a shot. If he's fast enough, he might even get in a second shot before his quarry bounds out of sight. Hill's advice to the archer is to learn to shoot fast. This does not mean to try to shoot faster than your normal rate of speed but to practice the technique of nocking, aiming, and firing in smooth rapid order until your normal rate of speed becomes greater and you can do it with calm efficiency instead of nervous hurry. Careful, deliberate aiming is okay on the target range, but for the hunter who deliberates too long in his aiming, it could mean an absentee target,

Hill swings quiver under his arm when crawling through low brush to keep arrows from catching.

Out in the open again, he reaches back with his left hand, pushes quiver up to normal position.

When searching for game, seek out and follow the animal trails. Look first for signs that indicate regular and recent use, then for tracks that indicate what species of animals are using the trail.

especially since, more often than not, that target is already on the move when the shot is being fired.

Hill makes a practice of periodically brushing up on his technique of drawing, nocking, aiming, and loosing arrows in rapid succession, to see if he is still doing it right or if he has developed any bad habits, like flinching on the loose or making some other mistake that is affecting his marksmanship. By following this practice, any archer can perfect his technique to a point where he will be able to shoot twice as fast with the same, if not more, accuracy. The trick is to start slowly but smoothly at first, drawing an arrow from the quiver, .nocking it, aiming and loosing it in one smooth unbroken motion. If you stop to aim too long, the rhythm will be broken. Practice bringing your arrow into firing position as you draw the bow so that when it reaches full draw it is already on target and ready for immediate release. Go through these motions in a smooth, unhurried cycle until you have become proficient not only in the mechanics of nocking and shooting, but in hitting your target as well. Once you have developed this rhythmic pattern of operation, you can gradually increase the speed to where the entire operation will become an instinctive maneuver and leave you free to concentrate on your target instead of technique.

Since wild game will rarely hold still for you, it is good to practice on moving targets, such as paper pie plates rolled down a hillside, or stacked corrugated cardboard targets slid down an inclined wire. Practice on targets moving at different angles toward or away from you as well as in broadside travel and vary the distances to develop your judgment. Learn also to shoot from a variety of positions, such as on one knee, down on two knees, from squatting and sitting positions, stooped over, etc., and with the bow held at every angle from the conventional perpendicular to horizontal position. Such practice will give you an advantage in hunting that can mean the difference between success and failure.

But, no matter how good a shot you become, success will elude you unless you are able to find the game and get those shots in. That means shedding all your civilized instincts and going back to nature, training every sense, nerve, and fiber in your body to act, walk, stalk, and think like an animal. To outsmart your quarry, you will have to learn a great deal of animal lore, know what your quarry eats, when and where he sleeps, what his habits are, and which of his three protective senses—sight, hearing, and smell—he relies on the most. Much of this can be gleaned from reading books on animal behavior, but one of the best

Having followed the trail carefully, Hill comes to a bare spot and picks up tracks of a coyote.

Sandy soil or loose dirt (with buck deer tracks, above) will often put you on the track of game.

ways to find out is to talk to professional hunters in your area, preferably men who hunt or trap full time rather than the average enthusiast who works in town and only hunts in his spare time. Indians who make their living as trappers are the best source of animal lore information, if you are lucky enough to find and befriend one. Howard Hill owes a great deal of his hunting success to what he's learned from Indians and the fact that he hunts like the Indians do.

"If you don't know what time of day your game is sleeping, where he sleeps, what time he feeds, and what and where he eats," says Hill, "why, then, you're just out in the woods walking around." The diet of a particular animal will often vary with the season and the locale. In the spring he may eat one thing, in the fall something else, and in the winter another thing. For instance, during the berry season, bear can sometimes be found in blackberry thickets, or huckleberry or blueberry patches. At another time of the year, you might find them by a stream catching salmon or trout, while at other seasons they may be turning over logs eating worms, grubs and similar bear delicacies. Wild boar will eat acorns when acorns are ripe, grass in the spring, and root worms when it's wet and the ground is soft. When the ground is dry and hard and there's nothing green around, he may go to where the ground is more or

less sandy and root up the grass roots which he finds sweet and succulent. With a basic fund of animal lore, you can hunt your quarry intelligently and stack the odds of finding him more in your favor.

"When hunting in unfamiliar country," says Howard Hill, "I try to devote the first couple of days to a reconnaissance, covering as much territory as I can without walking too fast, and following more or less a straight line without bothering to hunt out every pocket. I'll follow along the ridges, covering from eight to 10 miles in one day, just getting the feel of the country and trying to locate the game, find out where it's feeding, where the water holes are, etc. Because at this point I'm trying to make time, I don't hunt quite as slowly, but follow the ridges where it's easier going and I can cover more ground.

"Once I know there's game around, I get down to serious hunting, moving much slower and hunting out every pocket thoroughly. At such times I won't cover over a mile or two at the most in a day. I'll take a few steps, then stop and look around. You should look more than walk when you're stalking and at no time should you go blundering through the woods. The Indian says, 'Walk a little and look a heap.' That's good advice. If you walk through the woods at a normal gait, you'll be telegraphing your approach to every animal in the neighborhood and they'll never let you get close enough to shoot an arrow."

The careful stalker steps forward on the toe of his foot, tenderly feeling the ground before setting his weight down. Each spot on the ground is carefully surveyed for possible dry leaves and twigs that would crack and send out an alarm before a foot is planted into it. Hill often uses his bow tip to move a twig or dry leaf out of the spot he intends to step into. It takes only one careless step to startle a deer and put an abrupt end to your hours of stalking.

Sometimes, when the ground is covered with dry leaves and your deer is in sight, the only thing you can do is stand per-

fectly still and hope that he'll come toward you. Watch him carefully, and when he walks, you can walk, too. If you synchronize your movements right, the noise he makes in the dry leaves will drown out the noise you make and let you work your way in closer to him without alarming him.

When searching for game, follow the ani-

At left, holding bow in one hand with arrow nocked and ready, Hill "walks a little and looks a heap" as he stalks.

Descending a slope, remove arrow from bow as safety measure. Unstable footing could cause fall, injury by arrow.

In still-hunting, archer picks a spot where game is likely to pass, conceals himself and waits patiently for action.

mal trails and look for tracks that indicate what animals are using the trail. Unbroken dry weeds stretched across a trail mean that no deer or large animal is using that trail. Such animals would break or push aside these weeds in their path. Study the dry leaves in the bottom of the trail. If they are crushed and broken, you can be sure that animals are using the trail. A trail that has whole unbroken leaves and, especially, large spider webs across it, is one that is not being used regularly.

If you follow a trail long enough, you'll come to a place where the ground is bare, or maybe sandy, with loose dirt that will have tracks in it indicating what kind of animal is using the trail.

"When I follow a trail," says Howard Hill, "I usually walk along one edge of it or just outside of it so as not to disturb any tracks that may be in it. If the trail is along a hillside and there's room enough to walk below it, I try to follow it that way. In this way, the trail is up closer to my shoulder level and I can study it better without stooping. If the trail is filled with leaves and no tracks, though, you might as well follow in it until you come to a bare spot that has tracks."

When Hill hunts an area, he'll work his way up a ridge, then, as he reaches the top of the hill and can see across to the opposite hill, he'll stop, steady his binoculars on his bow tip and carefully scan the opposite hillside for game. Then, he'll move up further to the crest of his ridge until he can look down and scan its opposite side. The best way to approach game on a hillside is to come downhill toward it because, during the day, thermals and air currents usually move uphill from the valleys and will carry a man's scent to the quarry if the man is below it.

For this reason, if Hill spots game on the opposite mountain slope, he won't follow a straight line course to it that would carry him down his slope to a point where he would have to come up to the game from below, but instead, he will take a circuitous route, going down the side of his slope, then up the side of the slope on which the game is until he reaches a point higher than the game. From there, he will move in sideways along the slope until he is directly above the animal and then stalk down toward it. Aside from putting the wind in your favor, stalking downhill is much easier and doesn't leave you too winded to use your bow with accuracy when the time comes.

"The closer you can get to game with a bow," says Hill "the better are your chances of bagging it. But it's also possible to get too close. I'd rather get a shot at an animal at, say, 40 yards when I have some cover, than at 25 yards with little or no cover. A deer may not see you at first, but the second you raise your bow to shoot, he's gone.

"It's better to select a spot with partial cover that will break up your silhouette and make you less distinguishable to the deer. Then, when his head and eyes are behind some brush or tree and he can't see you, you've got a chance to raise your bow and shoot. I try to wait until he stops and starts feeding, because then he's looking at what he's eating and less likely to see me. But if he should look up and see me, I freeze and hope he'll think I'm a stump.

"Some people say that no animal can see you when you're sitting perfectly still. Well, I disagree. I think a lot of animals know the silhouette of a man whether he's moving or not, and I think the color of the clothes you have on has something to do with it. Some say they can't tell color. Well, maybe not, but they certainly can tell the difference between white and green, or some other bright color. You can hide behind a bush wearing a green or camouflaged shirt and an animal will come a lot closer to you than if you had a white shirt on. Of course, it's a lot safer to wear a bright red shirt, especially during the gun hunting season, because there are a lot of hunters who can tell red from green a lot

easier than they can tell man from beast, and you're less likely to be mistaken for a deer if you wear a conspicuous color.

"When moving in on an animal, I try to use my judgment and get as close as possible without sacrificing cover. I don't want too much cover because I still have to shoot through the brush, and when an arrow leaves a bow, it doesn't travel in a perfectly straight position until it's about 60 or 70 feet away. For the first 40 to 60 feet before it straightens out, its feather end is swaying from side to side and needs plenty of room to pass through the brush without touching any of it. I say a man needs a 15-inch diameter hole in the brush to shoot through for the first 50 feet. If he doesn't have it, he won't get an arrow through it one in six times."

When the ground is covered with dry leaves, even an Indian can't stalk close enough to kill with a bow. At such times, it's best to "still hunt." In still-hunting, you pick a spot where game is likely to pass, hide yourself and wait. When the game comes by, you shoot. A good place to still-hunt is near a water hole that animals use, on a trail that leads to and from the feeding areas, or where trails cross. Study the spot from a distance to learn what time of day the animals pass by, then on the following day, get there early, find some place of concealment, clear away all the dry leaves and twigs from your hiding spot, and settle down for a long, quiet wait.

Once he's scored a hit, Hill waits for a while before going after wounded game. Normally animal will retire a short distance and bleed to death.

If you've picked a spot that overlooks the approaches from which the game will come, you'll have the time to ready your shot before it comes into range. Of course, you should make sure that your hiding place is downwind from the direction the animals will come or they'll know you're there long before they get within range and you'll just be waiting for nothing.

If there's no natural cover to hide in, you can build a blind, but make it look natural. A few tree branches and brush set so that you can raise up and shoot over it from kneeling position will make a good blind. Try to blend your blind into the natural setting so the animals won't notice that anything's been changed. Natural grass, broom sage, and just tree branches make good blinds if the trees are not full of leaves that would wilt too fast. You can make a tall blind to stand and shoot through by setting tree branches into the ground. However, if your blind is a conspicuous one, the animals will be suspicious and stay away. The best thing then is to build it and go away from it for a few days. This will give the animals time to become accustomed to it, inspect it, and satisfy themselves that it's not dangerous. Once they've accepted it, they'll pay no more attention to it and you can come back and use it in a few days.

Often, when Hill has stalked an animal and finds that he can't get any closer to it because of dry leaves, natural obstacles, or open country that would expose him to his quarry, he uses a ruse to startle the animal and drive him in to closer range. He fires a special arrow which he has devised, sending it high over the animal to fall to the ground behind it. On impact with the ground, an explosive cap in the arrow head, such as is used in toy pistols, goes off with a bang. Very often the animal will almost run Hill down in its race to get away from that spot.

This explosive arrow, which Hill always carries in his quiver for such emergencies, is tipped with a metal tube that has an oval opening in one side to load the cap, and a sliding pin-hammer in its nose which is pushed up against the cap upon impact with the ground. Before Hill devised this "spooking" arrow, he accomplished the same ruse by shooting a blunt into the air. The explosive arrow, however, with its loud report, is a much more effective spooker.

Driving animals into range is another effective hunting technique when a group of hunters go out together. The hunters will split up into two groups, one group stationing itself along runways or passes and waiting while the other group fans out and drives the deer toward them. The drivers don't have to whoop it up; in fact, the deer will move ahead of them just as well, if not better, if they stalk the deer in careless fashion. The deer should always be driven downwind so they don't

Tracking wounded deer, Hill finds arrow caught on shrub. Blood, deer hairs clinging to feather indicate that arrow passed through animal's body.

Hill looks for blood drippings, which leave an easy-to-follow trail. It is sportsman's duty to track down and finish off any wounded animal.

WRONG way to remove arrow from tree. Twisting shaft to loosen arrow will only break the shaft.

CORRECT way to remove arrow is to cut away bark and wood from around broadhead, then . . .

pick up the scent of the hunters who are lying in wait for them along the trails.

You can't always count on deer running away when they see you. Some species, like the blacktail and the mule deer, will often hide and let you come very close to them, then sneak off when you've gone by. "I've had that happen to me often," says Hill. "I'd be walking back to camp, anxious to get in before dark, and making plenty of noise (by hunting standards), when, through the corner of my eye I'd spot some portion of a deer that's hiding in the brush alongside the path I'm traveling. In such cases, the best thing to do is keep right on doing what you're doing, maintaining the same gait and noise level, walking a little to the right and then to the left, gradually working your way in closer to the deer. Never look straight at him or stop to stalk him because the minute he knows you've seen him, he's off. He'll watch you and figure that you don't see him, and if you work it right, you can get in close enough for a shot before he realizes what you've been up to."

When stalking a trail, it's also a good idea to look back frequently. Often, you will stalk right past a deer that hears you coming and stays hid in the brush until you pass. Then he'll get up and sneak off. However, if you make a practice of looking back occasionally, you've got a good chance of spotting these wise ones and getting a shot in before they get away.

The characteristics of game vary with the different locales and have to be hunted by different methods accordingly. If you've been hunting deer successfully in Florida and then decide to hunt deer in Maine, you'll find that you can't hunt the Maine variety in the same manner as the Florida breed. That goes for any type game in all parts of the country. The thing to do, therefore, when you decide to hunt a new and unfamiliar locale is to get the lowdown on the game habits of that locale from local hunters and trappers first. Then, with what information they give you and the experience you've had in other locales, you'll be better fitted to hunt the new area.

As mentioned before, the arrow differs from the bullet in that it kills by causing hemorrhage whereas the bullet kills by shock. Therefore, the trick is to place your broadhead where it will cut through the most veins and arteries and thus kill more quickly. A chest shot is desirable because it not only causes internal hemorrhaging but also the collapse of pierced lungs. A deer's heart is located low and up forward in the chest cavity where it is protected by the lower portion of the shoulders. The best way to pierce the heart with an arrow is to hit the deer just above and slightly back of the shoulder rear joint where the heart is protected only by ribs and muscle. This, of course, takes expert marksmanship and ideal shooting conditions. If the deer is facing you, you can reach his heart and lungs by hitting him in the small depression where the shoulders

... using pliers, and the handle of the knife as a lever, the loosened broadhead is worked free.

curve inward and the neck begins. Neck and spine shots are also fatal. An abdominal shot will cause less hemorrhaging and take much longer to kill a deer. It should be avoided whenever possible.

Once you've hit your deer, sit tight. Don't go chasing up to the spot or you'll spook that deer clear into the next county. A deer, when hit, will take off and run to get away from the spot where he was hit. He doesn't know what hit him and if he doesn't hear anyone following him, he'll soon stop and figure he's eluded the enemy He'll then lie down and within a comparatively short time, depending on where he's been hit, quietly bleed to death. However, if the hunter follows after him immediately, that deer will keep on going despite his wound and put enough distance between him and the hunter to make tracking him a long and difficult task.

Generally, an archer can see where he's hit a deer before that deer jumps out of sight. The only thing to do then is to sit down very quietly and wait for a half hour to an hour before making a move toward finding the deer. This is one of the most difficult parts of hunting and requires all the self-control you can muster to resist the urge to chase out after the animal. During this time, the deer, after seeing no one is following him, will lie down and, if not dead when finally hunted down, will be too sore and stiff to move fast.

If you're not sure whether you hit the deer, wait about 15 minutes, then carefully stalk up to the spot where he was standing and study the ground for signs of blood. If you locate the arrow and it has blood or some deer hair caught in its feathers, you can be sure you've scored a hit. A broadhead will often pass right through an animal's body and, as the animal tears through the brush, the arrow's protruding barbed head will catch on a twig or branch and pull right out of the animal's body. If you find a clean arrow stuck in the ground or a tree, and no signs of blood along the deer's trail, you can be fairly certain you missed him.

Having made a hit, it is your duty as a sportsman to track that animal down and finish it off if it hasn't been vitally wounded. Never, under any circumstances, should you give up the hunt and let a wounded animal go unattended. The person who commits such wanton destruction is violating the principles of true sportsmanship and has no business being a hunter.

After you've given your animal enough time to settle down and succumb to his wounds, your job is to find him. This calls for expert tracking, especially if you've hit him in a spot where he's done more internal bleeding than external. Search the ground for signs of blood and possible footprints indicating the direction in which he's gone. Never follow on top of his tracks. If you walk in them, you may pass one and not see it, then if you have to check back, that track may have been stepped on and obliterated. Often, due to a change in the light or angle of vision, a track you missed seeing at first will show up clearly when checking back. If you've given your quarry enough time to settle down, and follow the tracks carefully, you'll have no trouble finding your trophy.

The bow hunter who goes after wild boar or bear is heading into dangerous territory and should know pretty well what he's doing if he wants to come out in one piece.

"Some say that if you let an animal alone, he'll let you alone," says Howard Hill. "Well, that may be true, but there's always an exception to the rule—and you just have to have one exception and you're not around any more. You might meet 20 grizzly bear and they all run, but the 21st might charge—or you might meet that one first, or third, or tenth. You have no way of knowing which one he'll be, so the best way to hunt any animal is to play them all like each one is going to be the exception.

"Of course," says Hill, "sometimes you take chances without knowing it. You're

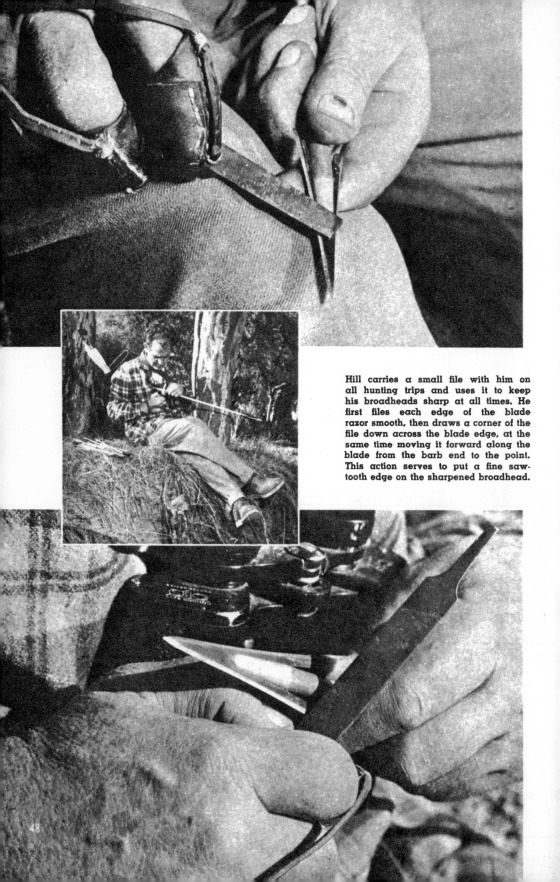

Hill carries a small file with him on all hunting trips and uses it to keep his broadheads sharp at all times. He first files each edge of the blade razor smooth, then draws a corner of the file down across the blade edge, at the same time moving it forward along the blade from the barb end to the point. This action serves to put a fine sawtooth edge on the sharpened broadhead.

48

going down a trail and the bear's coming up. Neither of you know the other's there until you meet at 20 or 30 feet. Then things start happening. If he's a grizzly and he charges, well then you'd better have said your prayers or have something to stop him with—and a bow and arrow isn't the thing. It takes a high-powered rifle to stop a grizzly and anyone who thinks different isn't likely to be around long to argue the point.

"It's very dangerous to meet an animal like that with a bow and arrow because you have no knock-down power. The grizzly is about the only animal in America that I ever worry about when I'm in the woods hunting. At certain times of the year, a bull moose can be dangerous, too. That's if you get between him and his mate during mating season. Any other time of the year, he'll run off if he sees you."

When stalking dangerous game in Africa, Hill carries a rifle and let's a bearer carry his bow for him. Then, when he spies his game, if he finds he can get in close enough to use his bow without being seen, he'll take the bow and use that. But, until then, he's not anxious to be taken by surprise with only a bow in his hands. Of course, if you have a good shot along with you, you can let him carry the rifle and cover you with it while you stick to the bow.

Wild boar are hunted with dogs and on horseback. When the dogs have the boar bayed, you dismount and get in your shot, being careful not to hit one of your dogs.

When a boar charges, Hill usually stands his ground and waits till the boar is about six feet from him. Then he lets fly an arrow aiming for the brain, and side steps the boar just as it takes its final leap at him. This requires precision timing, much the same as a bullfighter uses. If you dodge too soon, the boar can turn with you, but if you wait for his final lunge, he's in mid-air then and can't turn with you.

If you've put an arrow into some species of dangerous game, it's wise to take a rifle with you when you set out to track him down. You'll need it bad if your arrow only wounded him and he's lying in wait for you.

In closing, remember that the greatest thrill in bow hunting is the hunt and not the kill. The kill is a badge of merit to prove your skill in stalking and wood lore, but the archer who succeeds in getting even a near miss is just as thrilled as the one who bags his game, for the test of a good hunter is not his marksmanship in hitting the target, but his ability to get within bow range of his quarry, a feat which the gun hunter with his long-range weapon is not called upon to duplicate. The best bow shot in the world won't bag a deer if he lacks the ability to find his quarry and move in to where his marksmanship can be utilized. So if you've taken a shot at a deer and missed, don't feel bad. Instead, celebrate, for you've proven yourself a hunter and, as such, you're bound to get a second chance. •

Hill sometimes resorts to explosive arrowhead to spook game in toward him. Pin hammer detonates paper cap when arrow strikes ground behind game.

Accessories carried by Hill: binoculars, pocket knife, file for sharpening broadheads, arrow-removing pliers, talcum powder for finger stalls.

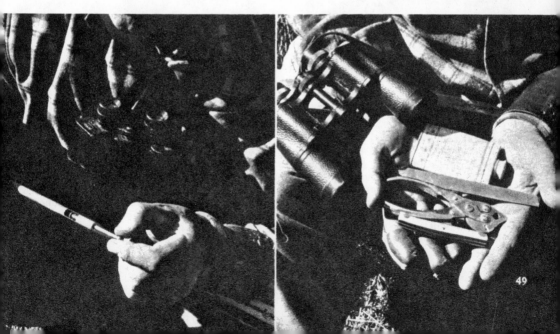

Fishing with Bow and Arrow

It takes more than a good eye to shoot fish with a bow and arrow. This is the supreme test of the bow hunter's skill.

Above, bow-hunter Howard Hill, aboard Errol Flynn's yacht "Sirocco," with three marlin shot by Hill, using broadheads attached to a rod and reel, in Gulf of California waters. At right, Bob Markworth, bow fishing for shark from Bill Carpenter's fishing boat "Pappy."

BOW fishing is an exciting sport that will test the archer's skill more than any other phase of archery. Your footing may be a rocking boat deck, or a pitching float, and though your quarry may be clearly in view beneath you, he's not necessarily where you see him, for the water plays tricks on the optics, bending light rays and giving you a false perspective. Besides this optical distortion, the water will deflect an arrow shot into it and thus add to the archer's aiming problems. On the credit side is the fact that your shooting range will be short, from 10 to 20 feet, rarely more, and since you are shooting down, there is no problem of trajectory. Also, if you can fish from a small bridge or pier, you'll have a solid footing with none of the pitching problems of boat or float.

Bow fishing of some sort is allowed in most states, but it's a good idea to check with your local fish and game commission

to see just what restrictions there are, if any.

Basically, there are two types and methods of bow fishing, for small fish and big game fish. For the small fish, a special reel attached to the bow is used to bring in the fish after it is speared. Large game fish, however, can't be handled this simply and, for these, the arrow is attached by line to a regular rod and reel. Once the fish has been hit, the bow is dropped and the fish is fought and landed with the rod and reel.

Bow fishing requires a different type of tackle than bow hunting or field archery. The fishing arrowhead has a hinged barb which lays flat against the point when entering the fish's body, then opens up to keep it from pulling out. The line is attached to this head. The head is only loosely fitted to the tapered shaft so that the shaft will drop off after the fish is hit, leaving the head and line attached to the fish. The shaft will float on the surface and can be retrieved later. Fishing arrows are not fletched, since the shooting distance is so short it wouldn't make any difference if the arrows had feathers or not.

For small fish that don't fight too hard, you can use one of the several bow reels available at archery shops. These are taped to the back of the bow, just below the hand grip, as shown in photos. The line, which is regular nylon fishing line, is fastened to and then wound around this reel. The lead is attached securely to the fishing head. To keep the line from throwing the arrow off in flight, run it along the shaft of the arrow and lightly Scotch tape it to the end near the nock. The line will cut through this thin band of cellulose tape after the fish is hit and the shaft comes loose. Once you've shot your fish, grasp the loose line and bring the fish in by winding the line back onto the bow reel.

Many types of fish can be lured to the surface, where they make good targets, by tossing bait on the water. Bait can be anything from bread crumbs to pieces of fish, chopped up crab, or chicken entrails, depending on the fish you're after and what they go for in the way of food.

However, it's one thing to lure a fish into view and quite another thing to shoot it with a bow and arrow. In aiming at a fish that is beneath the surface of the water, you must take into consideration such mechanical and optical obstacles as light refraction, optical illusion, deflection of arrow, and water resistance—not to mention that fish can move pretty fast when they want to. It takes a great deal of practice to overcome these obstacles and become a good bow fisherman. As a rule of thumb, your point of aim should be as far under the fish as the fish is deep in the water. The angle at which you're shooting must also be taken into account. Some fish will be farther out than others, requiring greater allowance for refraction and deflection, while fish directly beneath you will require a minimum allowance. Also, as water slows an arrow down considerably, use a heavy enough bow to reach and pierce the fish. Bow-fisherman Bob Markworth uses a 50-lb. bow for big game fishing, but for small fish your bow can be as light as 35 lbs.

Out on the high seas, shark is good game to hunt with bow and arrow. Sharks can be spotted easily by their high dorsal fins which stick up out of the water when they swim near the surface. To lure them into

Bob Markworth, using a 50-pound bow, above, sends arrow into baited shark. Once shark has been hit, Bob takes over rod and reel, right, to land prize.

bow range, cut up some bait fish—mackerel make a good bloody mess and blood attracts sharks—and toss it into the water. Blood meal used for fertilizer can also be spread over the water to attract sharks.

Sharks will come pretty close to the surface and make excellent targets. Use a heavy line on your arrow and attach it to a good, sturdy fishing pole. You can set the pole in a rack alongside you or let an assistant hold it while you shoot. Before you shoot, let out about 15 to 20 feet of slack on the line to reduce the resistance on the arrow as much as possible.

For a real fight, there's nothing like shooting a line into a marlin. Howard Hill has shot marlin in Mexican waters with a Lily-iron broadhead attached to a rod and reel. The marlin were lured into bow range with a Zane Grey Teaser and an outrigger with a skip-bait on it. Marlin will come up to the teaser, then run over to try

Archer Bob Markworth and victim, landed by reeling in heavy line attached to fishing arrowhead.

Arrow used in bow fishing has hinged barb which keeps the arrowhead from pulling free after hit.

53

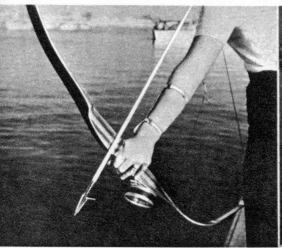

Above, rig for shooting small fish: bow reel is taped to bow just below hand grip; line is attached to fishing arrowhead. Since shooting distances are usually short, fishing arrows, as at right, are not normally fletched. Barbed fishing head, below right, is detachable; arrow shaft comes free after fish is hit, floats on surface of water. Fish is brought in by hand on line which is taken up on bow reel.

for the skip-bait which just skims along the top of water. The first marlin of the group pictured was killed instantly by a hit in the brain, which was not what Hill wanted. With the other marlins, Hill aimed for a spot under the dorsal fin and was rewarded by hours of battling before he landed his catch. One marlin landed itself by spearing its way through the planking of a small skiff, its long sword-like nose piercing through both sides of the boat, securely trapping the fish between the shattered planks.

If you're shooting from a pitching boat deck, take a shooting stance with feet spread well apart to balance yourself and bend your knees in time with the rocking deck, moving in rhythm with it to keep it from throwing you off balance. Keep an eye on your quarry and get a mental fix on the spot you want to use as your point of aim. Time your draw so that you can shoot at the exact instant when the boat has dipped its lowest and is just on the verge of pitching up again. If you time it right, there will be a split second when the boat will be practically motionless and you'll have a chance to aim and shoot.

Bow fishing adds that extra something to the sport of fishing that makes it an exciting and thrilling event. •

At left, instinctive archery champions Jo McCubbins and Leslie Speaks shoot fish from pier. Inset shows arrow loosed by Speaks striking fish.

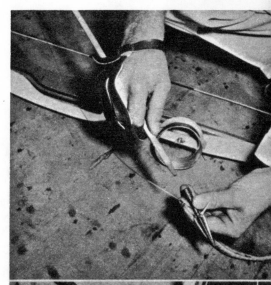
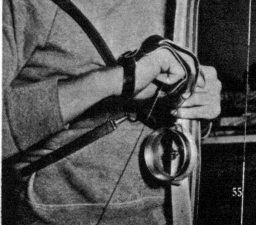

JOE FRIES
◀ **national target archery champion**

Four current national champions use bows designed by this expert craftsman and holder of two world's archery records.

Joe Fries, using a bow of his own design and the high corner-of-the-mouth anchor, demonstrates his target shooting stance, at left. At right, bull's-eye proof of the accuracy which has won him so many honors.

Herbert Dallinger Photo

Joe Fries of Glendale, California, has won the National Target Archery Championship two years in a row, 1955 and 1956. He has held the California State Target Archery Championship since 1952 (four years running). He holds the world's record of 1,039 points in the National Mail Tournament Field Round, and the world's record of 1,013 points in the York Round. His business is making custom bows of his own unique design. In the 1956 National Field Archery Tournament, three of the top winners used Joe Fries bows: Jo McCubbins, National Bare Bow Champion in women's division; Leslie Speaks, National Bare Bow Champion in men's division, and Peggy Ortez, National Woman's Free Style Champion. Joe, of course, won the National Target Championship with one of his own bows, making four winners in all using Joe Fries bows.—*L. H.*

DURING the 5½ years that I've been shooting, I spent a lot of time studying different types of bows and learning how and why they shoot. From this study, I set out to design a bow that would combine the stability and accuracy of the straight-limbed longbow with the speed and cast of the recurve. The result is the Joe Fries bow, which in 1956 won for its users four national championships.

My bow has a minimum amount of recurve to give it speed without sacrificing stability. I make up the difference in stress by lengthening the middle section, which gives me shorter limbs. In effect, I have a longbow with the stress characteristics of a short bow, but without the string pinch of a short bow. Other bowyers stress their bows by curving the backs more. That gives you cast but the bow is trickier. I have just enough recurve so the string doesn't wrap around the bow but hangs free like on a straight-limbed bow.

My bow is 5 feet 6 inches long between nocks with a 26-inch center section. It weighs 48 lbs. and is a center shot. I prefer center-shot because then the spine of the arrow is not so critical. The arrow doesn't have to curve around the bow so much and this lets me shoot a weaker spine with the same accuracy.

My draw length is 28 inches but I use a 27-inch arrow and draw it back one inch

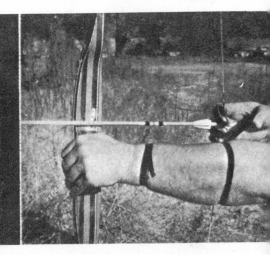

Joe Fries' draw length is 28 inches. He uses a 27-inch aluminum arrow and draws it back one inch into the bow. The inch difference in arrow length gives him the advantage of shooting a lighter shaft with a stiffer spine. When he draws he always looks at tip of arrow to make sure he's drawing it to the same distance.

At left, right way to grip bow: loosely, with hand turned outward at slight angle. Above, wrong way to grip bow: bow should not be held in tight fist as shown here.

At right, above and below, Joe Fries demonstrates high cheek anchor and release. In smooth follow-through, hand moves back slightly rests on cheek until arrow hits.

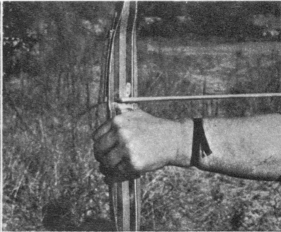

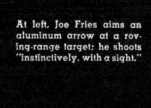
At left, Joe Fries aims an aluminum arrow at a roving-range target; he shoots "instinctively, with a sight."

At right, Joe Fries and the running buffalo he killed, with one broadhead arrow through the heart, for TV.

into the bow. That inch difference in the arrow gives me the advantage of shooting a lighter shaft with a stiffer spine—and every little bit counts in competitive target archery. I use aluminum arrows made by Easton Archery Shop of Los Angeles.

When I shoot, I use a loose grip on the bow, letting it jump forward in my hand on release. I use a sight for everything, even hunting; but I use it only as a guide. The sight is my secondary aiming point. I focus my eyes primarily on the target and aim instinctively, then check my sight to see if it's on target, too. In other words, I aim as if the sight weren't there, then check to see if it's where it should be—and it usually is, right in the middle of the target. Other archers use their arrow as the secondary aiming point. I use my sight that way because it gives me a finer check. My secondary point of aim will be right on target instead of under it. You might say that I shoot instinctively with a sight.

When I hunt, I use three sight pins: one set at 20 yards, one at 30 yards, and one at 40 yards. If my game is 10 yards off, I aim a little low with the 20-yard pin, and if it's 50 yards off, I aim a little high with the 40-yard pin. Beyond 50 yards, I don't shoot. This sighting system gives me all the distances and I'm always in line because the pins are in line.

I've hunted wild boar, sharks and buffalo with this system and found it very satisfactory. On the boar hunt, I took six shots at three pigs and scored six hits, four of them running. The buffalo was shot for a TV movie, as were the other hunts, and I killed it with one arrow through the heart. It was a running shot at 30 yards and I used a cut-down Bodkin broadhead arrow. It was a 2,300-mile trip to Wyoming just to shoot one arrow and come back.

While most target archers use the low chin anchor, I prefer the high corner-of-the-mouth anchor because it brings everything in line more. In the old days, they had to use the low anchor in order to reach a target at 100 yards, but with today's faster bows, you can move your anchor up higher and still sight in on your target. When I draw, I always look at the tip of my arrow to make sure I'm drawing it to the same distance every time. With my bow, one-half inch is equal to one pound and that can vary my arrow from two to three feet at the target.

I don't practice very often, but when I do, I mean it. I never shoot unless I feel like shooting and can do my best. I work toward consistency, trying to do everything in exactly the same way every time. When you do that, you're bound to shoot a good score. •

HOWARD HILL

◀ world's greatest bow hunter

**Howard Hill's tackle and shooting technique
are specially tailored for hunting wild game
where the archer has to be split-second fast.**

AFTER 32 years of shooting wild game all over North America and in the wilds of Africa, it's inevitable that I should develop a technique peculiar to my own method of operation, and a preference for certain types of tackle that work best for me. My archery is confined to hunting wild game where you have to be fast and accurate, making split-second decisions and acting on them even as you're making them. There's no time to take the conventional archer's stance, deliberate on whether your target is 30 yards away or

Veteran bow-hunter Howard Hill, shooting at high target, left, from kneeling position, below, demonstrates high cheek draw, using tooth as anchor.

60 yards, and dawdle with your aiming. Wild game just won't hold still for such maneuvering.

Because of this, I like a bow that is consistently dependable under all the diversified conditions of the hunt. Personally, I favor the straight-end longbow, not less than 5 feet 9 inches in over-all length, or 5 feet 8 inches between nocks. A fair amount of backset to add speed is all right, but not too much. I make all my own bows, of split bamboo and Fiberglas face and back, by an intricate process I've developed and patented. I shoot an 85-lb. bow for all ordinary game, a 100-lb. bow for rhino and buffalo, and a 110-lb. bow for elephant, drawing a 28-inch arrow on all three of them. I believe in using a bow as heavy as I can pull without strain, because of the faster, flatter trajectory of such a bow, its greater range and greater penetration.

I don't like the recurve center-shot bows because, for me, they're too sensitive. They have a tendency to exaggerate slight errors to the point where you can miss your target entirely. For instance, if you're shooting at a deer 30 yards away and you should happen to flinch a little with your left hand when loosing, well, with a straight-end longbow, you'll still kill the deer. But with a recurve, you won't even touch him—there's that much difference in the sensitivity between the two bow types. The same is true with a right-hand mistake. If you flinch letting go and move your string the least bit, as little as ¼ inch to the right or left with a recurve, that tiny error will be exaggerated enough to make you miss the animal. The same error with a longbow wouldn't throw you off enough to be out of the killing area at 30 yards.

It's true that a recurve gives you greater speed and cast with less weight, but in hunting, it isn't the cast that's going to do the killing, it's the accuracy. It doesn't matter how fast an arrow is traveling if

Howard Hill's rapid-fire shooting technique: bow hand moves to support bottom of quiver while right hand reaches for an arrow; having selected an arrow, bow is brought forward and arrow is nocked; by the time bow is elevated to shooting position, it is at full draw; the release is nearly instantaneous. Hill draws, aims and releases with one continuous unbroken motion. Total time between shots: 1½ seconds.

it fails to hit its mark. Over the past 32 years, I've tried all types of bows: window bows, semi-window bows, recurve, short recurve, working recurve, flair-backs, etc. I've made them myself and shot bows that other archers have made. I've tried to hunt with them and finally discarded them all because, for me, they're not as accurate as a straight-end longbow. In hunting you're shooting from all kinds of unorthodox positions, with the bow held at various unpredictable angles. Your game is practically always on the move, and with the high tension and excitement of making the kill you're bound to flinch once in awhile. At such times, I don't want to miss my mark because of a supersensitive bow that will exaggerate my slightest error.

When I shoot, I bring my bow and arrow up to my target from the low position I carry it in while stalking, rather than down from above as most target archers do. In this way, my bow moves only a short distance to full draw position, while the other way, it would be going up, then down, to get on target. My way is not only faster but much less conspicuous and not as apt to spook the game as is the other method. I'm also less likely to tangle my bow in overhead branches.

I use the high or cheek draw instead of drawing low as a target archer does, because this brings the arrow closer to my eye and reduces the angle drawn by the eye line and the arrow line by about 50 percent. Consequently, I only have to guess half the distance I would if I were using an under-the-chin anchor, thus reducing by 50 percent my chance of making a mistake in aiming. Because of this reduced angle between the eye and the arrow, I don't have to aim more than a few feet below my target, regardless of how close it is, and since I use a heavy bow with a fairly flat trajectory, I don't have to elevate above my target unless it is a considerable distance away.

To make sure I draw to the same spot each time, I use my last lower jaw tooth as my anchor. This works fine for me and reduces the chances of deviation in the length of my draw.

My method of aiming is known as the split-vision or secondary aiming method. It consists of fixing my eye on the spot I want my arrow to hit, then selecting an imaginary secondary aiming point several inches below the target mark (depending on the distance of my target), and without taking my eye away from the main target spot, bringing the point of my full-drawn arrow up until it is aimed at the secondary

target. To use this method of aiming, you have to practice seeing with your side or peripheral vision. One way to do this is to fix your eye on a definite mark and, without moving it away from that mark, point your arrow at various other marks located around it. Although your eye is focused on the main mark, you can still see the arrowhead without looking directly at it, and with a little practice, you'll be able to aim that arrow at any imaginary point without taking your eyes away from the main target. Once you've trained yourself to use your side vision in this manner, it is only a matter of practice on targets at various distances to determine how low and at what point your imaginary secondary aiming point should be.

By using this method of split-vision aiming, if an archer misses on the first shot, he can quickly correct for the second shot by shifting his imaginary aiming point the same distance to the right, left, up or down as the first arrow missed its mark. This provides a concrete means of compensating for mistakes which the instinctive shooter doesn't have. I have found this method, after years of using it in hunting, to be much faster and more accurate than any other method, including the sight and instinctive methods. •

JO McCUBBINS

women's national bare bow champion

From novice to champion in six months. No telling what will happen when Jo McCubbins settles on an ultimate shooting technique.

Jo McCubbins started shooting in early 1955 and within six months won the California State Field Archery Tournament in the woman's instinctive division by 170 points. She holds the National Field Mail Tournament record of 715 points, the highest score any woman archer has ever officially shot, beating the old record by 24 points. In 1956, she won the National Field Archery Tournament to become the current National Woman's Bare Bow Champion. So new is she in the field of archery that she still hasn't settled on a definite draw length but uses an arrow cut slightly longer than the 26 inches she currently draws to while developing her ultimate shooting technique.—*L. H.*

WHEN I became interested in archery early in 1955, Bob Bennett of Pro Archery in Costa Mesa, Calif., taught me the pure instinctive method of shooting and I've never used any other method since. Instinctive shooting is a challenge to me, and, as yet, I've had no desire to try shooting with a sight or space picture. Maybe that will come with time—trying out other methods—but right now I prefer the bare bow method.

When I shoot, I look at the target and concentrate on it. I draw without seeing the arrow or anything but the target. I don't try to judge the elevation or distance. I just aim instinctively, the way you would

At left, Jo McCubbins demonstrates the instinctive shooting form that has made her a champion. Below, nocking the arrow: arrow is twirled to bring up cock feather at right angle to string, then moved forward and back to engage string at nocking point; drawing fingers are then hooked around the bowstring.

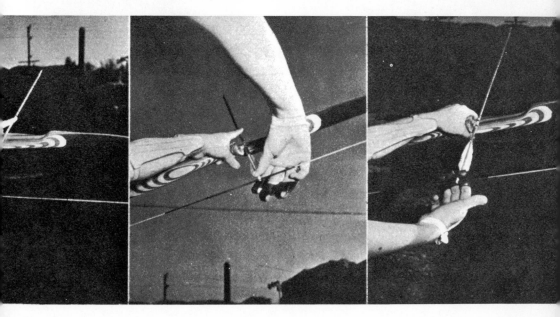

point your finger to indicate an object. Whenever I catch myself looking at my arrow, even out of the corner of my eye, it throws me off.

Lots of archers like to estimate the distances and then shoot, even when shooting instinctively, but I don't even like to do that. It doesn't help me. Not the way I shoot. I aim by "feel," not by using a sight or a space picture. My eye is focused only on the target center. I sense the distance to the target without knowing or trying to estimate it in feet or yards. By instinct, I aim higher for the more distant targets and lower for the closer ones. It takes a lot of

practice to develop this instinct, but once you have it, you can hit anything within range without wasting too many arrows to first get that range.

I use the high corner-of-the-mouth anchor because it's better for instinctive shooting. My bow is a Joe Fries bow, 66 inches long and weighing 35 lbs. I use all-aluminum arrows for tournament shooting because of their consistency in weight, spine, and straightness. My draw is 26 inches but that may still change if I should change my drawing technique. A person can vary his draw length up to a couple of inches by thrusting forward more with his

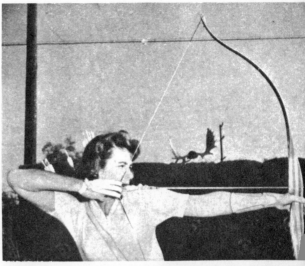

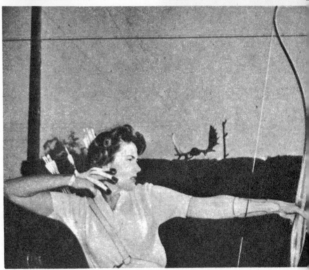

At far left, Jo McCubbins takes a comfortable drawing stance at right angle to target and nocks an arrow.

Bow is then raised to vertical position, above, and arrow is drawn back with first joints of fingers.

At full draw, upper right, Jo's elbow forms a straight line with arrow. Jo uses high corner-of-mouth anchor.

At right, in follow-through, Jo's drawing hand remains at cheek until arrow hits target. Note loose bow grip.

left hand or moving his head back or forward a little. Until you've settled on the most comfortable drawing stance, you can't really know what your correct draw length is. For this reason, even though I currently draw to 26 inches, my arrows are cut a little longer so that in case I change my technique a little and increase the length of my draw, I wouldn't be likely to pull the arrow back off the arrow rest and jab it into my bow hand.

Eventually, when I settle down to one fixed drawing stance, I'll have my arrows cut to the right length for that stance and that will be my regular drawing length.

When my instincts tell me that my arrow is aimed at the bull's-eye, I relax my fingers from the string, and see the arrow only when it hits the target. Until then, my eyes are fixed only on the target and stay there until the arrow hits. I never try to follow the arrow in flight as this would mean taking my eyes off the target for that split second of release. Such a practice would upset my concentration on the target and affect my aim.

I've found instinctive shooting very useful in hunting and have shot small game such as rabbits, and once, a skunk! The skunk cost me a good arrow. •

BOB MARKWORTH

exhibition trick shot archer

With a human life at stake, there is no margin for error in Bob
Markworth's spectacular performance with bow and arrow.

Photos by Milt Svensk

So precise is Bob Markworth's marksmanship that his assistant, Jan Jefferies, holds the small balloon and plaster disc targets at which he shoots unflinchingly during the amazing stage performance, Miracle Arrows.

Bob Markworth is a stage performer who shoots targets from the heads and hands of beautiful girl assistants. This act, which Markworth calls, "Miracle Arrows," has been performed on stage and TV and, although it is definitely *not* recommended for archers, however skillful, to use live people as targets, the techniques of archery employed by Markworth in his sensational act are well worth reviewing and can prove very helpful to other archers.—*L. H.*

WHEN a human life is at stake, you can't leave anything to chance. My act is one in which a girl entrusts her life to me and where the least bit of carelessness or over-zealous chance-taking can destroy that girl in one horrible split-second. Before I embarked on this stage career, I practiced continuously until I could hit an object the size of a mothball at 30 feet with fair regularity. I shoot about 150 arrows a day in practice, putting better than 90 per cent of those arrows in the center of a three-inch bull's-eye at 30 feet. Since my shooting distance on stage is always 30 feet, that's the distance I use when practicing.

I started shooting a bow and arrow in 1950, using a regular lemonwood bow, but soon moved up to a Kodiak Bear Bow and from that to a Smithwick (which I use in all my stage work now). I found that by using a sight I could improve my accuracy, and within four months, I was doubling my scores. I was the California Junior State Archery Champion from 1951 to 1953, and held the California Men's Quadruple American State Championship in 1953. I also hold the Southern California Broadhead record (shooting with hunting arrows under hunting conditions), with a score of 995, and have a Robin Hood Award, given through the courtesy of the Hugh Rich Archery Shop in Glendale, Calif., only to those who have split an arrow that was previously lodged in the bull's-eye.

I use a 40-lb., 5-foot 9-inch Smithwick bow for my stage work because I find it

At far left, Bob Markworth's finale: a blindfold shot, for which he is completely masked with a hood, spun around, and then left to shoot a balloon mounted directly over his assistant's head. He locates and aims at the target by following directions given by the girl. At right, Bob aims at a balloon held under the chin of assistant Marjean DuVol.

very well adapted to my exacting needs. It has a smooth release—the shock being absorbed into the thick handle—terrific cast, and a flatter-than-average trajectory. Because I can't take the chance of a bow breaking during my act, I replace my bows every three months. I use an extra-long bow, because the longer the limbs the smoother they relax on release, and hence, the smoother the release.

My draw length is 28½ inches and I use all-aluminum arrows because of their machine-precision quality; identical weights, spines, and straightness. There is no margin for error in this business.

Although precision marksmanship is an absolute must in my work, an equally important requirement is the power of intense concentration. I attribute my success in this field 50 per cent to marksmanship and 50 per cent to concentration. When I'm shooting a balloon out of a girl's mouth, I concentrate only on that balloon. I don't see the girl or allow myself to become aware of her presence and proximity to the target. If I should think of the girl and allow my mind to dwell on the consequences of a miss, I would become nervous and unable to shoot with any guarantee of accuracy. Only by blotting her out of my mind and focusing all my attention on the target can I be completely relaxed and sure of myself.

Before I developed these powers of concentration, I read books on the Yogi, Shinto, Hindu, and Rosicrucian ways of life. These impressed me deeply and although I never became fanatical in any one respect, I have taken certain practical aspects of each way of life and applied them to my archery.

Thus, when I shoot, I am completely oblivious to my surroundings and the fact that a live girl is holding my target. I feel, too, that having a very small target is actually an aid rather than a hindrance to me because I can concentrate that much more on a single point. Using this power of concentration, I once put 12 arrows in a row (shooting and removing them in sets of four so as not to split any) into a one-inch diameter circle at 30 feet.

To eliminate as much of the danger as possible in my act, I actually apply mathematical formulas to my shots, figuring out on paper just what the odds are on the possibilities of my missing a shot, and, having worked out a good safe formula, I abide by it. For instance, there are many shots I could make like shooting a cigarette out of a girl's mouth or a Ritz cracker from between her fingers, but these are too dangerous and would bring the odds too close for safety. For the sake of the sport of archery, and the safety of my subjects, it would be extremely unwise to take such foolhardy chances, however spectacular they would be in an act.

A much safer but equally spectacular stunt I pulled once was to challenge the best pistol shots of the Glendale Police Force to a contest, a friend and I shooting arrows against their bullets on their 25-yard pistol range. We shot about 60 arrows to an equal number of their bullets—and beat them by 13 points! It was a somewhat red-faced police force that read of the account in the next day's papers.

My current plan is to open an archery school in Glendale, Calif., and teach field and target-style archery, as well as hunting and fishing with the bow and arrow. •

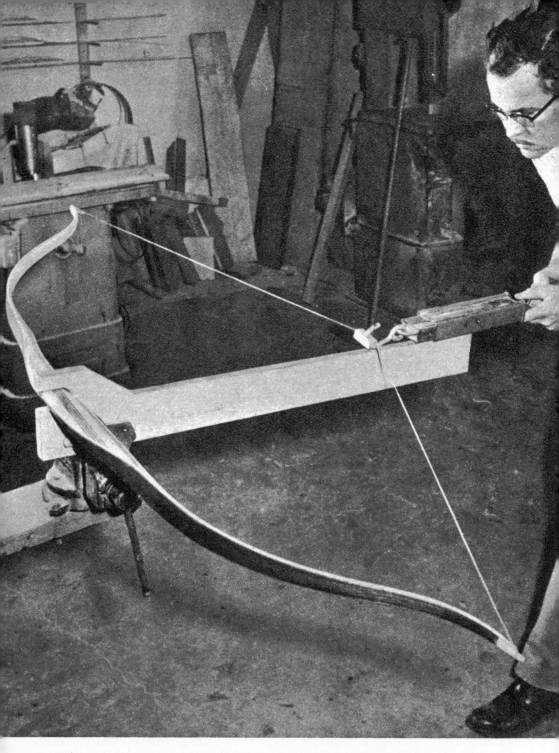

Tom Jennings of S. & J. Archery checks the weight of a finished laminated recurve bow with spring scale and graduated base board. Glass and core lamination thicknesses largely determine weight of each bow.

How to Make
a Recurve Bow

The knowledge gained through the experience of making your own bow makes this more than just a prideful accomplishment.

SOONER or later the enthusiastic archer gets a yen to make his own bow. His reasons may be economical or experimental, but whatever they are, his skill as a craftsman should be equal to his enthusiasm or his venture into bow-making could prove dismal and costly. It's one thing to get a slat or stave of lemonwood and whittle out a simple bow that will perform to a fair degree of satisfaction, but the beginner who attempts to make a laminated recurve bow is tackling the most difficult project in the critical field of bow-making. There are so many variables and pitfalls in the construction of a laminated bow that to turn out a successful job on the first try is an achievement in itself. Yet, the thrill of accomplishment and the knowledge gained through this experience make it a worthwhile venture, even if it takes two tries to succeed.

Today's modern bow is made up of laminations of wood and Fiberglas, the wood serving as a neutral core or spacer between two laminations of Fiberglas. Actually, it is the Fiberglas that does the work of the bow, carrying 88 percent of the load while the wood core carries only 12 percent. As you increase the spacing between the two Fiberglas laminations by using a thicker core, you automatically increase the strength of the bow by the square. Thus, if you double the thickness of the core, you increase the weight of the bow four times. Since the thickness of the laminations is measured in thousandths of an inch, it is easy to see how just a few thousandths of an inch more thickness in the core can make a bow too heavy for your use.

There are several woods that are suitable for bow-making, among them hickory, Osage orange, yew and lemonwood. However, maple is the most common core wood used in glass-faced and backed bows because it is a consistently hard, dense wood, very straight-grained, and readily available in good clear grades. The beginner is wise to use maple rather than some of the other woods which are tricky to handle because of knots and twisty grain patterns.

To make things easier for the beginner, there is a bow kit available that con-

Core laminations are cut from same block of hard maple in order to insure matched limbs.

Kit contains all materials needed for making laminated recurve bow in weight desired.

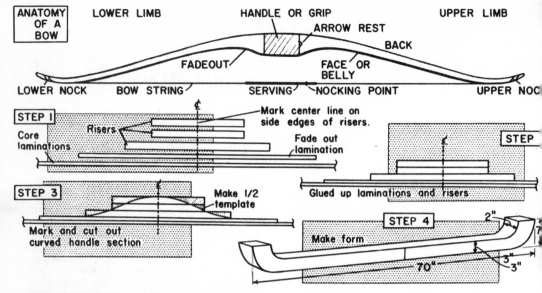

LOWER LIMB   HANDLE OR GRIP   UPPER LIMB

ARROW REST

BACK

FADEOUT   FACE OR BELLY

LOWER NOCK   BOW STRING   SERVING   NOCKING POINT   UPPER NOC

STEP 1

Core laminations

Risers

Mark center line on side edges of risers.

Fade out lamination

STEP

STEP 3

Make 1/2 template

Glued up laminations and risers

Mark and cut out curved handle section

STEP 4

Make form

2"

70"

3"
3"

Glue up risers and base core laminations; clamp unit to straight bar to insure good glue lines.

tains all the necessary woods, Fiberglas and glues to make a custom, 5-foot 6-inch recurve bow. The wood sections and Fiberglas strips are of uniform thickness and the wood is cut from matched sections of hard maple wood of the finest quality. The kit, which sells for $24.95, is put out by S. & J. Archery, 10945 Burbank Blvd., North Hollywood, Calif., makers of custom Smithwick bows, and provides all the necessary materials to make a custom bow, as shown in the photos in this chapter.

Before making a bow, however, it is a good idea to acquaint yourself with the anatomy of a bow and the terms used to denote its various parts. As shown in the diagram on this page, the bow, when held vertically, has an upper and lower limb, each extending from the central handle or grip. The smooth ledge cut into the upper part of the grip on the side where the arrow will travel is called the arrow rest or plate. The side of the bow facing away from the archer is called the back, while the side facing the archer is called the belly or face. The belly portions on either end of the handle that taper inward toward the limbs are called the fadeouts or dips. At the end of each limb is a string groove which is called the nock, known respectively as the upper and lower nock. The bowstring has a reinforced center section called the serving; the little ball of string located opposite the arrow plate and used

After glue has dried, clean off edges of bow assembly and lay out curve it is to be cut down to.

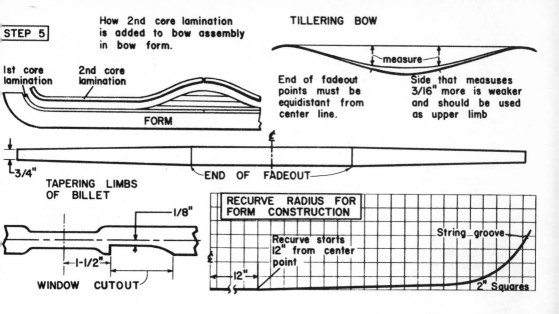

How 2nd core lamination is added to bow assembly in bow form.

1st core lamination

2nd core lamination

FORM

TILLERING BOW

measure

End of fadeout points must be equidistant from center line.

Side that measures 3/16" more is weaker and should be used as upper limb

3/4"

END OF FADEOUT

TAPERING LIMBS OF BILLET

1/8"

1-1/2"

WINDOW CUTOUT

RECURVE RADIUS FOR FORM CONSTRUCTION

Recurve starts 12" from center point

String groove

12"

2" Squares

to take the guesswork out of nocking the arrow is called the nocking point.

To make the custom bow shown in the photos, you will need the following materials, all of which are supplied in the bow kit mentioned above, and can be purchased as a unit or as separate items:

2 strips Fiberglas ($1\frac{3}{4}$x36) ....for belly of bow
2 strips Fiberglas ($1\frac{3}{4}$x36) ....for back of bow
4 lengths Canadian hard maple lamination ($1\frac{3}{4}$x36)
....for core of bow
1 length maple lamination ($1\frac{3}{4}$x28x$\frac{1}{4}$) ....
.................base lamination to be faded into core
1 maple block ($1\frac{3}{4}$x18x$\frac{1}{2}$) ....
.... for riser, or center section of bow
2 maple blocks ($1\frac{3}{4}$x14x$\frac{1}{2}$) ....for top of riser
2 maple blocks ($1\frac{1}{2}$x$\frac{3}{4}$x$\frac{1}{4}$) ....
....................for string groove reinforcement
1 bottle M-74 plastic glue ....
.....................for cementing glass to wood
1 bottle C-31 plastic hardener ......used on glass only
1 bottle Urac No. 185 ......for cementing wood to wood
1 bottle Urac hardener ....
......................................for all wood-to-wood surfaces

The thicknesses of the glass and core laminations determine to a large extent the weight of the finished bow and should be carefully selected with that in mind. It is practically impossible to draw up a formula that will give you the correct thicknesses for any specific weight bow because of the many other factors that can affect your bow weight. For instance, your bow weight will be affected also by the length of the bow, the design and amount of recurve, its width and taper, and the type wood used in the core. A long center-section riser

Use a band saw or jig saw to cut out this curve, taking care not to cut into fade-out lamination.

will shorten the working limbs and increase the weight of the bow, while a shorter grip section will allow you longer working limbs and thus lighten the bow. It takes very little to add or subtract 10 pounds from the weight of a bow and, for this reason, anyone building a laminated bow of his own design can never be sure what weight it will be until he can actually test the bow.

Bow makers make many bows and do a considerable amount of experimenting before they establish a standard of operation for any one bow, and because this has been done with the Smithwick Custom Bow, it is possible to order a bow kit for the weight bow you wish to make. The kit will then have laminations of the correct thickness to give you the right basis from which to start. Even then, the success of your ultimate weight goal will depend on how skillfully you shape and taper the limbs. Once the billet or roughed-out bow is completed, you cannot add any more weight to it. You can only take weight off.

As a general rule, the following lamination thickness specifications will, if applied to the bow design shown, produce a bow that will correspond closely to the desired weight you wish to achieve: for a 50 lb. bow: .175-inch core, .050-inch back glass and .060-inch belly glass; for a 40 lb. bow: .175-inch core, .042-inch back glass and .048-inch belly glass; for a 25-30 lb. bow: .160-inch core, .040-inch back glass and .045-inch belly glass.

The lighter 25-30 lb. bow is usually a lady's bow and requires additional changes in the tapering of the billet to bring the weight down without reducing the thickness of the limbs too much. This is because there is a ratio between the thickness and the width of the limbs where the bow gives the best performance.

With all your materials laid out, you are now ready for the first step in making your bow. This step consists of gluing the riser blocks to the core laminations. However, before applying any glue, it is a good idea to assemble the component parts dry and familiarize yourself with the position each piece occupies so that there will be no mistakes when the glue is applied. Once the glue has been applied, you must join and clamp the pieces together without delay in order to get a perfect bond. To make sure that the pieces are positioned properly, mark the center line across the side edge of each piece. When all units are assembled, the center lines should coincide to form a straight line across the edge of the risers.

In this first step, you glue together only the three riser blocks, the fade-out lamination, and one pair of core laminations. The pair of core laminations are laid end to end under the riser blocks to form a continuous 6-foot long core as shown in the diagram. This core comes in two sections; in order to assure perfectly matched upper and lower limbs, two 36-inch lengths of core lamination are cut from the same 36-

Taper fadeout into base lamination. Extreme care must be taken to avoid gouging base lamination.

End of fadeout blends into base lamination. When done right, there won't be any detectable ridge.

Glue second pair of core laminations, Fiberglas facings to bow assembly and secure to bow form.

Inner-tube strips or tape can be used to secure assembly to bow form to establish recurve shape.

inch long block of hard maple. The two pieces, coming from the same section of wood, are as closely matched in grain and wood characteristics as is possible to achieve. This is true also of the second pair of core laminations which are glued to the assembly in another operation.

The wood portions can be cemented together with any good wood glue, such as urea-base glues or Elmer's Glue. The glue supplied with the kit is Urac No. 185, which is used with a Urac hardener. Apply the glue evenly with a 1½-inch brush to both surfaces being joined and clamp the assembly firmly between blocks and a straight bar of wood or metal. The straight bar is important for insuring good glue lines. Use enough clamps to distribute the pressure evenly along the entire area being

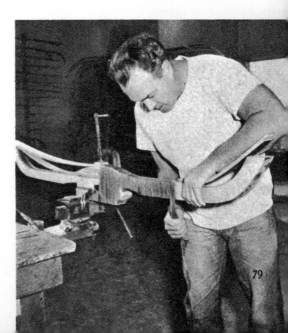

Glued bow assembly is clamped to steel form and dried in heating chamber in professional set-up.

Howard Hill dries his bows with heat of a blow torch directed into improvised drying chamber.

glued. Allow 24 hours drying time, the first six hours at at least 100 degrees Fahrenheit. A closed car in the summer sun will usually get at least this hot. Another trick is to wrap the glued assembly in a sheet of canvas that has been treated for water-proofing and let this lie in the direct sun. The heat will build up in the canvas wrapping to a very high degree. Howard Hill improvises a drying chamber by wrapping a length of 10-inch stovepipe with asbestos, closing it off at both ends, but leaving a small enough opening at one end through which to direct the heat of a blowtorch.

While the assembly is drying, make a wooden form for shaping the billet. This form should be bandsawed out of a 2-inch thick solid wood block that is seven inches wide and 70 inches long. In the absence of solid wood, plywood can be used by laminating two lengths of ¾-inch and one length of ½-inch plywood together to build up the 2-inch thickness required. Cut the form out to the shape shown in the diagram, making sure that both ends of the form cut out are identical in shape. The best way to assure this is to make a template, from heavy cardboard or thin sheet metal, of one half of the desired shape, then trace this onto the form block, first on one end of the block and then, flopped, on the other end of the block. The form, when cut out, should be perfectly square to insure a firm even base for clamping the glued laminations. After cutting out the recurve contour, draw a line on the form parallel to

After drying by heat at recommended temperature, bindings are taken off and billet is removed from form. Billet will have taken recurve shape. Clean and square up both sides of the billet by sanding.

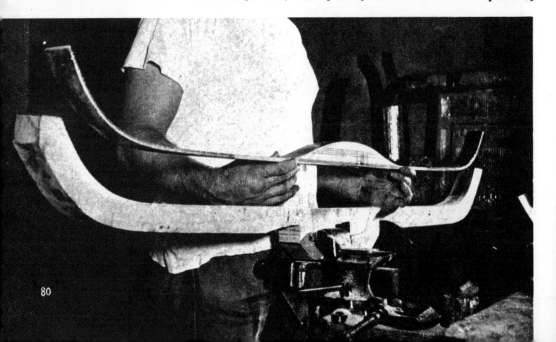

this shape and spaced three inches from it and cut away the excess wood along this line. The precision and evenness with which you make this form will determine the quality of your finished bow to a great degree.

After the bow assembly has dried, clean the excess glue off both sides of the riser section and then lay out the curve it is to be cut down to as shown in diagram (Step No. 3). Since both sides of the riser section fadeouts are the same shape and equally distant from the center line, a half template can be used in both positions to trace the curve onto the riser section. The fadeout *must* be a very gradual curve into the base or core lamination. This is essential to the final tiller of the bow.

Use a band saw or jig saw to cut out this curve but do not cut into the fade-out lamination. The gradation of the fadeout is too critical an operation to be done with a saw. It should be done by careful sanding, preferably using a drum sander, until the fadeout gradually blends into the core lamination. Be very careful not to cut *into* the core lamination or leave even the slightest ridge at the end of the fadeout. Cutting into the core lamination will weaken the bow at that point, while leaving a ridge will stiffen the limb, add to the bow's weight, and interfere with the bow's performance.

The next step is to glue the second pair of core laminations to the bow assembly. This operation is performed in the bow form in order to establish the recurve shape. The

Cover outer Fiberglas surfaces with masking tape for protection and to facilitate marking layout.

Using a flexible tape measure or rule, establish the center of the bow, taking care to be precise.

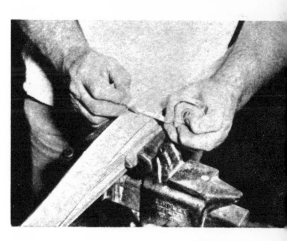

Now draw two center lines on the bow, one crosswise and the other lengthwise. All measurements should be very carefully made as even a slight error will be reflected in the accuracy of the finished bow.

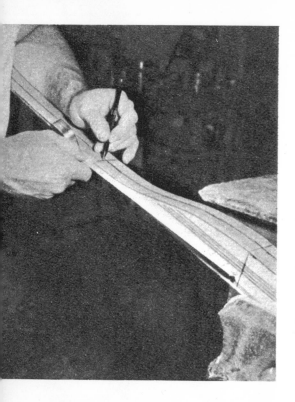

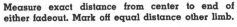

Measure exact distance from center to end of either fadeout. Mark off equal distance other limb.

Mark off bow tips for required width, then lay out limb tapers from end of fadeout to bow tip.

best way to do this is to set the two strips end to end and secure them together temporarily with masking tape across their outer surfaces. Then apply glue to the inner surfaces of both strips and the back surface of the bow assembly. Now join the laminations together, centering the taped joint with the center line on the riser section and lining it up with the center line on the bow form. Do this in the form, using a C-clamp on the center line to clamp the assembly to the form. Then, starting at the center point and using loops cut from an old inner tube, numerous clamps or masking tape, secure the laminations firmly to the form. To facilitate removal of the billet from the form, wax paper should be placed between the form and the laminations. Also, because the rubber loops and tape, when tightly wound around the assembly, exert most of the pressure on the edges of the laminations and very little in the middle, a spacer strip, consisting of a strip of wood $\frac{1}{16}$ inch thick and $\frac{1}{8}$ inch narrower than the laminations, should be laid along the top of the billet and centered to leave a $\frac{1}{16}$-inch margin along each side before the tape or rubber

loops are wound around the assembly. This spacer strip will equalize the pressure exerted over the entire surface and insure a good glue line. No glue is applied to this spacer strip.

As you work your way toward the bow tips, the laminations will be forced down into the form and will take the shape of the curve cut into the form. Do this along both ends, securing the entire length, then set the form into a hot place to dry. Because extreme heat may melt natural rubber, loops preferably should be cut from one of the synthetic-type tubes which are more heat resistant. Dry the billet at no less than 100 degrees F. When the glue dries, the laminations will retain the shape of the form. Clean off the excess glue from the sides of the core and, with No. ½ grit sandpaper, clean off any wax that might have transferred to the core from the wax paper.

The next step is to apply the Fiberglas to the bow assembly. The Fiberglas is obtained in two thicknesses, the heavier strips being used on the belly of the bow and the lighter ones on the back. Rough the sides of the glass to be glued (either side can be

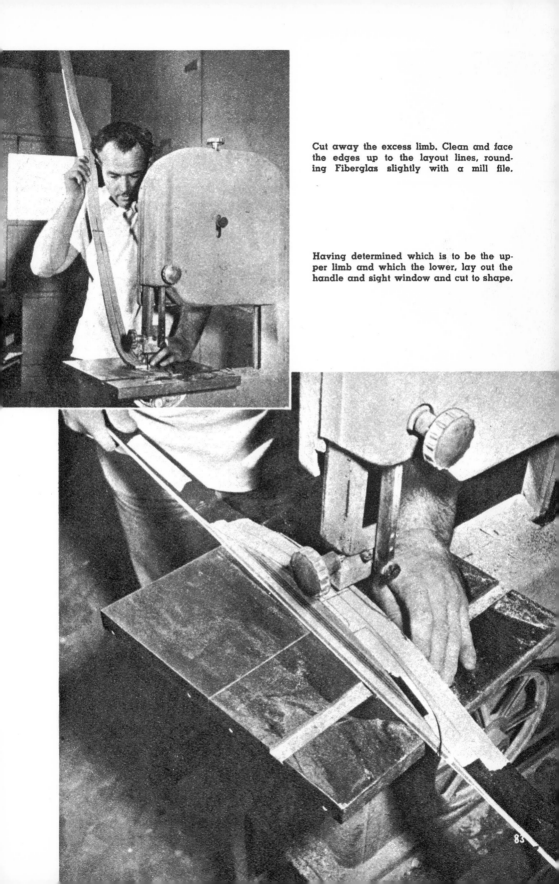

Cut away the excess limb. Clean and face the edges up to the layout lines, rounding Fiberglas slightly with a mill file.

Having determined which is to be the upper limb and which the lower, lay out the handle and sight window and cut to shape.

Following the photos on these pages, rough shape the bow handle, on a disc sander if you have one.

Curve top surface of the arrow rest slightly so that shaft does not rest on too broad a surface.

used) with very coarse sandpaper, preferably using a drum sander, to remove all the glaze. Do not be afraid to sand.

Next, join the two strips of back glass end to end with masking tape applied to the side opposite the one roughed up for gluing and lay this glass, rough side up, into the form. The wooden bow assembly then sets in on this, and the belly glass, joined end to end with masking tape like the back glass, is set on top of the whole assembly. This is a "dry run" to make sure that all the component parts are properly sanded and ready for gluing. It is a good idea to cover the outer surfaces of both the back and belly glass with masking tape. The tape will keep the glass clean and provide a surface for measuring and marking off the limb tapers to be cut later.

Now, using M-74 plastic glue and C-31 hardener, apply glue to the roughened glass surfaces first, then to both sides of the wood core, using a 1½-inch brush. Plastic glue and hardener should be applied *immediately* after they are mixed. The glue is mixed four parts adhesive to one part hardener by weight. Add the hardener to the resin and stir for five minutes. The maximum time you can allow the mixed glue to set in the pot is five to 10 minutes.

However, once it is spread on the laminations and glass, you have 30 minutes to join and clamp the pieces together. Glue surfaces must be absolutely free of moisture.

After you've glued the surfaces, set them into the form with a spacer strip laid across the top as was done when gluing the second pair of laminations to the first, and after lining up the center mark with the one on the form, use a C-clamp over the center mark to hold the assembly to the form. Then, as was done before, wrap the billet tightly to the form with loops of inner-tube rubber or masking tape, starting from the center point and working your way toward the tips. The glass will take the shape of the curved form as you carry the wrappings outward. Be sure to save some of the plastic glue and hardener (in unmixed form) for the tip blocks. Dry the billet with heat of at least 120 degrees F., but not over 140 degrees, for six hours, then let harden for another 48 hours. Important: this glue will not function properly without observing the stated degree of temperature.

You now have the completed billet. Clean and square up both sides of the billet with very coarse sandpaper, using your disc sander. Leave the masking tape on the bow for use in marking the layout. Now draw

Final shaping is done with files. You can shape the sighting window to your own requirements, there being no hard rules concerning the location of the window or the depth to which is should be cut.

two center lines on the bow, one lengthwise and the other crosswise. From the crosswise center line, measure the distance to the exact end of the fadeout on one side and draw another crossline at this point. Then measure an equal distance on the other side of the center line and draw another line across the bow belly. These lines at the ends of the fadeout will mark the points from which the bow limbs begin to taper toward the tips.

Next, at the tips of the bow, measure ⅜ inch from each side of the longitudinal center line. This will give you ¾-inch wide bow tips. Now draw diagonal lines from these bow tip marks to the outer ends of the fadeout cross lines and you will have the correct limb taper as shown in diagram. For a 25 to 30 lb. lady's bow, the billet, which is normally 1⅝ inches wide, should be narrowed down on a disc sander to a width of 1½ inches and the limb taper should end up with ⅝-inch-wide tips instead of ¾-inch.

After marking off the limb tapers, cut away the excess limb along these lines and then clean and face the edges up to the layout lines. Round the glass slightly on the face and back with a mill file, but do not go to too much trouble because these limbs

are rough width at the tips and will be changed when the bow is lined up.

Next, locate the points for the string grooves by measuring 33 inches each way from the center line with a flexible tape or rule, letting the rule follow the curve of the bow along the belly. Use a small round rat-tail file and file the string grooves ⅛ inch deep on both sides of the tip, rounding them off slightly to prevent their cutting the tillering string.

You are now ready to string the bow for tillering. The tiller is the shape of the bow at strung position. Use a string with large loops for the tillering string. After stringing up the bow, check its limbs for evenness by sighting along the string from tip to the middle of the main part of the limb as shown in photo. If the recurve twists to one side of the middle of the limb, remove material on that side and refile the string groove on that side. Repeat this process until the recurve is in the middle of the main part of the bow.

After the tips are in line, sight along each side of the limb and file out any bumps you may see. In doing this, you may change the tiller of the bow, so check frequently to see that the recurves do not take on an off-side twist. If they do, you can correct it by tak-

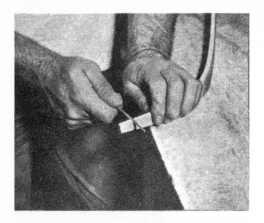

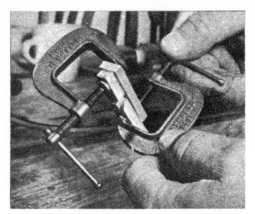

String grooves, ⅛ inch deep, are filed into both sides of each bow tip using small rat-tail file.

Glue tip blocks to bow tips over string grooves; Fiberglas should be well roughened before gluing.

Shape bow tips to the contour of the bow limbs. File string grooves into tips with rat-tail file.

Finishing off the bow, file string grooves along the recurve on belly side of each of the limbs.

ing off sufficient material from the side to which the limb twists to even out the limb.

Before the handle can be shaped out, you must determine which limb will be the upper limb, since the upper limb should be weaker than the lower limb. This is because when drawing the bow, you will be exerting more palm pressure below the center line on your grip, as well as putting more tension on the lower half of the bow string due to having two fingers below the nock of the arrow and only one above it. To equalize this, the lower limb of the bow should be a little stiffer than the upper limb, and you determine this by measuring the distance between the bow string and the limb curve at the point of the fadeout on both limbs. The points along the limbs at which you take this measure should be equidistant from the center line of the bow. The weaker limb should then measure $\frac{3}{16}$ inch more between limb face and string than the stronger limb and this limb should be used as the upper limb. If it measures less than $\frac{3}{16}$ inch, you can lighten the limb by rounding the face glass slightly.

Having tillered the bow and determined which is to be the upper limb, you can now mark the handle for the grip and window cutout as shown in diagram, lining it up so that the window cutout is on the upper limb. Cut out the handle as shown in photos with files and disc sander; round out the handle and sight window to the desired shape as shown in diagram. You can shape this to your own taste, there being no hard and fast rules concerning the location of the sight window and the depth to which it

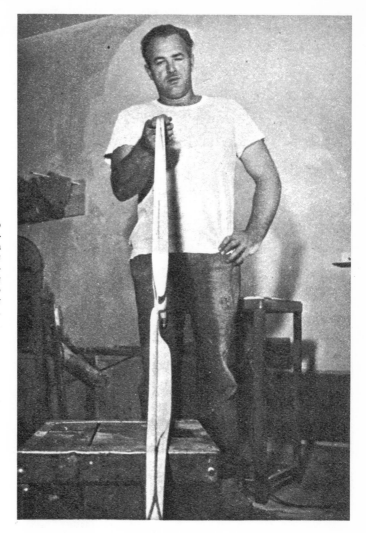

String the bow and check the limbs for evenness by sighting along the bowstring from tip to tip. If recurve tends to twist to one side, correction can be made by removing additional material from side to which limb twists, refiling string groove on that side.

should be cut. However, it should not be cut to a depth greater than ⅛ inch from the longitudinal center line as shown. This sight window should be cut on the left side of the bow (as bow is seen by archer when shooting) for right-handed shooters, on the opposite side from that shown in the diagram for left-handed shooters. File a slight curve into the top surface of the arrow rest so that the shaft does not rest on too broad a surface when shooting.

Finally, cement the tip blocks to the bow tips over the string grooves. Finish off the tips by shaping them down to the contour of the bow limbs and filing the string grooves into them with a rat-tail file.

Your bow is now ready for sanding and painting. Sand to a fine smoothness and paint with clear varnish or lacquer.

SOME FINAL TIPS:

1. When removing masking tape, strip from center of bow out toward tips so as not to lift any glass splinters along the edges. Use care.

2. When filing bow, always file toward glass to avoid chipping.

3. Before any clamping, always have a "dry run" before applying glue.

4. Remember, you must use heat to cure this glue right.

5. Glass surfaces to be glued must be roughed thoroughly.

6. Extreme care should be used in fadeout to avoid gouging base lamination or have fadeout end too abruptly.

7. Do not get impatient to shoot bow before it is finished. •

How To Make Bowstrings

You won't save a *lot* of money making your own bowstrings, but your bowstrings will be ideally tailored for individual bows.

Anchor thread under clip and wind required number of turns around peg and nails. Each turn of thread is brought around next inside pair of nails.

After winding the required number of turns around the nails, hold the threads down and cut the ends by running the blade of a knife between the nails.

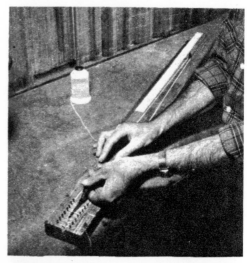

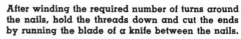

Hold down the threads with one hand and gather the loose threads at one end. Wrap twice around index finger to keep them from slipping out of line.

Fray square-cut ends of thread about one to two inches back by scraping them with a knife blade or pulling them across teeth of a hacksaw blade.

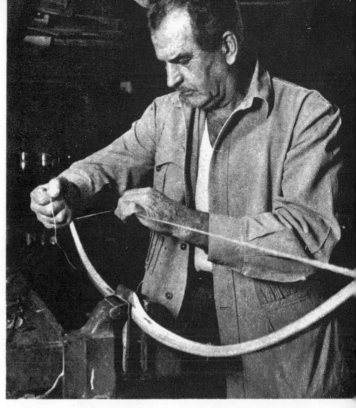

Basic materials needed for bow-string-making include: spool of bowstring thread, serving thread mounted on a serving bracket, a sharp knife, beeswax. At right, Howard Hill, who makes all his own equipment, puts serving on a bowstring in his home workshop.

THE part of your equipment that takes the most abuse and wears out the fastest is the bowstring. Your bowstring should always be in top condition if you want your bow to last. Should a. string break at full draw, the sudden release on the limbs of your bow may easily cause them to break. A good bowstring sells for $1.00 to $1.50, but you can make your own for as little as 20c worth of materials. With such economy, you can afford to keep several bowstrings on hand and discard old ones before they reach the danger point of wear.

There are three preferred materials used in bowstring making—dacron, fortisan, and linen—each of which has its advantages and disadvantages. The best way to decide which is best for you is to try them all. Dacron, because of its higher abrasion resistance, is a very fine material with which to start.

Besides the dacron bowstring thread, you will need a spool of serving thread, which is a heavy glazed-finish cotton thread, a cake of beeswax with resin mixed into it, and a sharp knife. These materials, designed specially for bowstring-making, are available at all archery shops.

Important considerations in making a bowstring are the length and weight of the bow. Each string must be tailor-made to fit a particular bow. As a general rule, the string should be approximately 3½ inches shorter than the length of the bow, measured from nock to nock. Its strength is decided by the number of threads used to make up the thickness of the string.

The two most popular bowstrings are the spliced loop and the endless or served loop. The former is composed of threads in multiples of three, while the latter is composed of threads in multiples of two. The guide used by Art Schampel of Hugh Rich Archery to determine the number of threads for various bow weights when using dacron thread is as follows:

FOR SPLICED LOOP STRINGS

Bow Weights	No. of Threads Per String
25 to 30 lbs.	9 threads
35 to 40 lbs.	12 threads
40 to 45 lbs.	15 threads
45 to 50 lbs.	18 threads
50 to 55 lbs.	21 threads
55 to 60 lbs.	24 threads

After fraying both ends, wax about 15 inches at each end, as Art Schampel of the Hugh Rich Archery Co. is doing here. Lay this strand aside and repeat the entire procedure two more times to make three identical basic bowstring strands.

To braid the loops, hold the three basic strands with the ends pointing toward you and twist them into a rope, starting eight inches from the ends.

The technique is to take the outside strand to the right, twist it away to the right, then bring it back to the left across the other two strands.

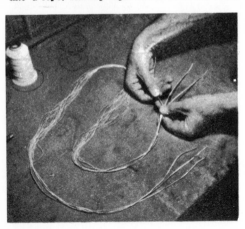

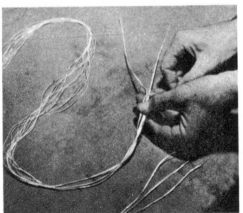

Repeat twisting operation, taking the outside strand to the right, twisting it to the right, then pulling it back across the other two strands.

Continue to twist, always taking outside strand and bringing it back over other two, until you have completed 28 turns (22 turns for lower loop).

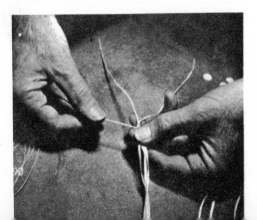

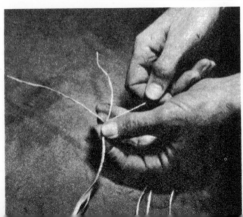

FOR ENDLESS STRINGS

Bow Weights	No. of Threads Per String
25 lbs.	8 threads
30 lbs.	10 threads
35 lbs.	12 threads
40 lbs.	14 threads
45 lbs.	16 threads
50 lbs.	18 threads
55 lbs.	20 threads
60 lbs.	22 threads

The lighter the string on a given bow, the faster the bow will shoot. But the string must not be so light as to make it too weak for the bow.

While a couple of nails driven into a flat surface will suffice for winding the strands in string-making, a jig, as shown in the photos, will work much better and insure accuracy. The jig for the spliced-loop string is made with a length of 2x4 fitted with nails and a peg as shown. Using a 5-foot 6-inch bow as a standard, the peg should be placed 37 inches from the first pair of nails, at the other end of the board. Move peg ½ inch closer to nails for each inch less than 5 feet 6 inches your bow is.

Two parallel rows of nails are set into the board, the rows spaced 1¼ inches apart and the individual nails spaced ⅜ inch apart. Provide six to eight pairs of nails. Between the two rows, cut a notch into the wood to serve as a channel for the knife blade when cutting the threads. A small metal clip fastened to one side of the nails will serve to anchor the end of the thread.

For the spliced-loop string, three basic strands are needed, each strand composed of one third of the number of individual threads required to make up the string. The string shown in the photos is a 15-thread string, therefore each basic strand is made up of five individual threads.

Completed rope twist at one end will look like this. Separate the three strands at each end of the rope twist for matching in the next step.

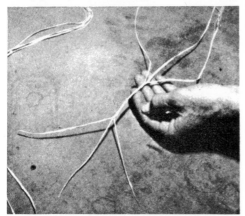

To fashion the loop, curve this twisted section around until separated strands above the twists match up with the strand ends below the twists.

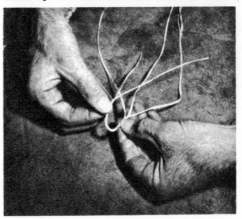

After matching, twist each pair of strands together, twisting always to the right. Now repeat rope-twisting operation with the three strands.

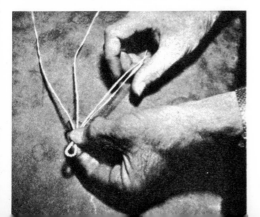

Rope-twisting can be facilitated by placing loop over hook and braiding under tension. Continue for 34 turns to complete the loop at upper end.

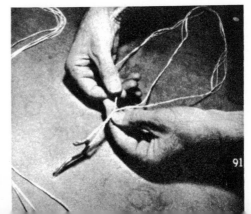

91

After completing the upper loop, untangle the strands above the braided end, pulling back with even tension along the full length of the strands. Holding all three strands under even tension, start rope-twisting 7¼ inches from the other end. Make 22 rope twists, then separate loose strand ends. At this point you can relax the tension on the strands and make the bottom loop, in the same manner as you made the upper one. Use hook to keep the lower loop under tension while braiding the three strands together.

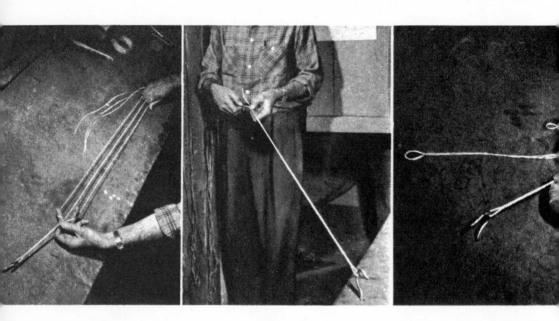

Make the basic strand by anchoring the end of the thread under the clip and winding it around the first set of nails and the peg, coming back and around the same set of nails to complete one turn. On the second turn, wind the thread around the second pair of nails, just inside the first pair. Repeat this winding operation as many times as you require threads in your strand—three times for a nine-thread string, four times for a 12-thread string, etc.—each time bringing the thread around the next inside pair of nails. This way, each thread is wound a little shorter, and when the ends are cut they will be of uneven lengths and thus taper more gradually into the string when twisted.

After winding the required number of turns around the board, hold the threads down and cut the ends by running the blade of your knife between the nails and across the threads as shown. Next, carefully gather the threads at one end and wrap two turns around your index finger to keep them from slipping out of line. Fray the square-cut ends of the threads about one to two inches back by scraping them with a knife blade or pulling them under

pressure across the teeth of a hacksaw blade. This will insure a smooth blend into the string when twisting the loops. Do this with both ends, then wax about 15 inches of the strand at each end. Lay this strand aside while you repeat the operation two more times to make three basic strands.

To twist the loops, hold the three basic strands with the ends pointing toward you. Twist them into a rope, starting eight inches from the ends (7¼ inches from the end for the lower limb since this limb should have a smaller loop). To twist, take the outside strand to the right, twist it away to the right, then bring it back to the left across both of the other strands. The middle strand will now be the outside one and this is given the same treatment: twist to the right and bring back to the left over the other two strands. Keep repeating this operation, always taking the outside strand on the right, twisting it to the right, and then bringing it back to the left over the other two strands. Make 28 twists for the upper loop (22 for the lower), then take out all the twist from the remaining ends of the strands.

To make the loop, curve this twisted

Next, with one loop anchored over the hook, untangle the string, separating the three strands through the unbraided center of the bowstring.

With strands separated, stretch string out and twist string to left for about 24 turns. A dowel through the loop will help to maintain tension.

Continue to hold the string under tension and wax the entire length of the string. Then rub the wax in and smooth it with a soft leather pad.

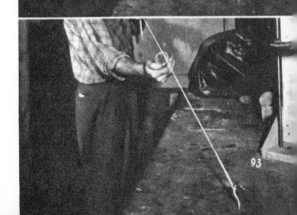

93

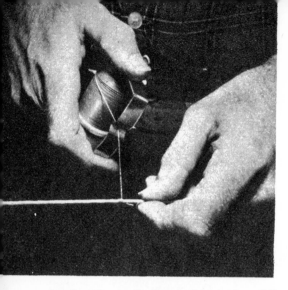

Put the string on the bow and serve the middle section of the string, starting two inches above the arrow rest and finishing six inches below it.

When proper tension is set on server, server can be spun around the bowstring rapidly to automatically wind the serving thread around the string.

section until the strand ends at the top of the twists meet the strands at the bottom of the twists. Make sure these match up properly, center strand joining with center strand, and outer strands joining with outer strands. The match is right only if the top strand that crosses over the adjacent two joins with the corresponding bottom strand that also crosses over its adjacent two. If two strands cross over one, that end is up-side down and should be twisted one turn to line it up properly.

When you've lined up the strand ends, twist the middle two together, then the outer pairs, to make a twisted loop terminating in three basic strands. Now follow the same twisting procedure with the three strands, taking the outside one to the right, twisting it away to the right and then bringing it across to the left over the other two strands. Repeat this for about 34 turns to complete the loop at one end.

Next, anchor the loop over a hook and, with your fingers, untangle the three strands below the twisted end, pulling back with even tension along the full length of the strands to separate and stretch them out evenly. Keeping the strands under even tension, start twisting them together at the other end, beginning about 7¼ inches from the end and twisting 22 turns into the strands.

At this point you can relax the tension on the strands and make the bottom loop in the same manner as you did the top one, curving the twisted section around and matching and joining the end strands with

the main strands as before. Then hook the loop over a hook and twist the remaining strands under it into a rope for about 34 turns to complete the bottom loop.

Now, with one loop anchored over a hook, stretch the string out and untangle the strands. Then put 24 twists to the left for the length of the string. Slip a dowel through the loop and pull hard on it to stretch it out, being careful to brace yourself in the event that the string should let go. However, if you've followed the directions, your string will hold.

Still keeping it under tension, wax the entire length of the string. Then rub the wax in and smooth it with a leather pad. Your string is now ready for serving.

To serve it, string it on the bow, then start winding the serving thread around the string, starting two inches above the arrow rest and finishing six inches below it. The serving is started by laying about ¼ inch of thread on the string, then taking three or four turns back over this thread, taking up the slack on the thread at the same time until the frame of the server is tight against the bowstring, the string fitting snugly into the V-notch of the serving frame. Now, spin the server rapidly around the string by cranking the bowstring in rhythm with the centrifugal force of the server. The server will automatically feed out the thread and wrap it tightly around the string. Tie it off at the end by running four or five turns of serving over a loop of scrap thread, then passing the end of the serving through the protruding loop and pulling it

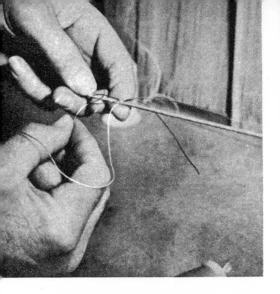

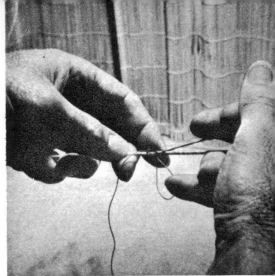

To tie off the end of the serving, serve four or five turns over loop of scrap thread, then pass end of the serving through the protruding loop.

With end of serving passed through loop, loop is pulled back out from under the serving, drawing end of serving thread back under last few turns.

back through and under the last turns with the scrap loop. Another method of tieing off the end is to run a large arc with the end of the serving thread and then wind four or five spirals of thread under this arc. Stretch the spiral straight along the string and take the arc of thread and wrap it around the string, winding it over the stretched-out thread for as many turns as the thread was spiraled. Then pull the end back through and cut it off flush with the string.

Finally, add the nocking point by wrapping a tiny ball of dental tape around the served string at a point where it will hold the nock of the arrow. To find this point, lay a square along the string and move it up until it lines up with the arrow rest of the bow. Then, mark a point ⅛ inch above the point where the square crosses the bowstring. Your nocking point can be either above or below this mark, depending on whether you want it above or below your arrow nock.

The endless string is much easier to make and requires far less skill. A board with two pegs or nails spaced a distance apart equal to the length of the string is all you need. (An endless string should be made ½ inch shorter than the twisted loop type.) A pair of pegs in the middle, staggered and spaced six to seven inches apart, will be handy for separating the strands and holding the string under tension when needed.

To make the endless string, start at one end and wrap the thread around the two

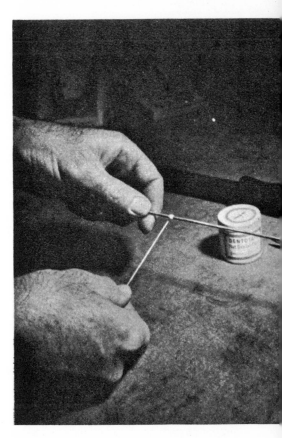

Add the nocking point by wrapping a tiny ball of dental tape around the served bowstring at the point where it will hold the nock of the arrow.

Making endless-type bowstring, Hugh Rich winds thread around two anchor points spaced out to equal desired length of string; each turn around anchor points adds two threads. After necessary number of threads have been wound around anchor points, ends are tied off with a square knot.

main pegs, taking as many turns as you require strands for your string. One complete turn equals two strands. Tie the ends off with a square knot, then spread the two sections apart, slipping half of the strands around one of the off-center middle pegs and the other half around the other peg. Now slide the whole string unit around the pegs to bring the knotted end over to the middle of the board where you can work on it. Over this knotted end, lay four to five strands of thread. Tie them down with serving thread for a length of about three inches. Tie off the ends of the serving thread and trim away any thread that protrudes from either end of the serving. This section will form your served loop at one end.

Remove the string from the middle pegs and slide it around the outer pegs until the served section is curved evenly around one of the pegs. Mark the other end with grease pencil for loop serving.

Move the string around all four pegs again and repeat the serving operation as before, adding four to five strands of thread to the string between the pencil marks and tying them down with serving thread.

Slide string around the pegs and place four or five short lengths of thread over the knotted end section and secure to string with serving.

Marked end is moved off peg and reinforcing procedure is repeated. Hugh uses two bobbins, doesn't tie off until completing final step.

Now, slide the string around the two main pegs until the served sections are curved around each peg. Pull their ends together and join them by tying them down with serving, running the serving four to 4½ inches down the string for a recurve bow, or just one to two inches for a straight-end bow.

Fold the string in half to mark the center section for serving, then wax it, twist entire string to the left three to four turns, stretch it back over the pegs, and serve the center section to complete the string.

If a string is too short or too long, it can be lengthened or shortened a little by twisting it to the right or left. •

After serving about three inches, tie off ends of the serving thread and trim away any excess. This section will form served loop at one end.

Reinforced loop section is slipped around peg anchor at one end. Pencil is used to mark section to be reinforced and served at the opposite end.

Reinforced loop ends are shifted around pegs and loops are joined by serving, about four inches for a recurve, two inches for a straight-end bow.

String is waxed, twisted three or four turns to the left, then served along the center section. Finish off by adding a nocking point as before.

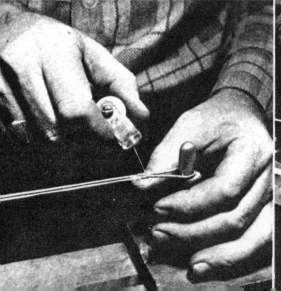

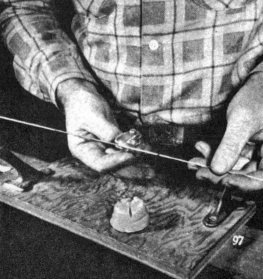

How to Make Matched Arrows

No bow, however well designed and built, can make an arrow hit its mark if that arrow is unbalanced and otherwise poorly constructed.

STRANGE as it may seem, the most important and critical piece of equipment an archer uses is not his bow but his arrow. The bow is merely the power that hurls the arrow into space, but it is the arrow that must fly straight and true to its mark, and no bow, however well designed and built, can make an arrow hit its mark if that arrow is unbalanced and otherwise poorly constructed. Yet, arrows of good, matched design can be shot with consistent accuracy even with a poorly balanced bow, for once the discrepancies of the inferior bow are mastered and compensated for, it will hurl each arrow with the same force and cast characteristics, putting the responsibility for accuracy on the archer's shooting technique and the arrow's flight characteristics.

Naturally, for a quiverful of arrows to behave in uniform fashion, it is necessary that those arrows be matched as closely as possible in wood, weight, spine, length, and shape. Without exception, every arrow should be as straight as a rule. The slightest bend or twist in the shaft will sabotage its accuracy. All the arrows must be fletched (feathered) in the same manner with the same type feathers and nocked *across* the grain (never with the grain). The making of a perfect arrow is one thing, but to make 12 perfectly matched arrows is quite another thing, requiring considerable patience, care, and skill.

Fortunately, it is no longer necessary to turn your own dowel shafts from rough lumber or measure the spine or stiffness yourself. Matched dowels of the proper diameter and spine can be bought in almost any archery tackle store, together with all the necessary tools and accessories for fletching, tapering, nocking, varnishing, etc., needed to make a set of good, matched arrows. The important thing is to know what your needs are, and this is determined by the length of your draw, the weight bow you use, and the type of archery you go in for.

Although there are several good woods such as Douglas fir, Norway pine, and birch, suitable for arrow making, the best and most popular is Port Orford cedar, a very straight-grained, strong for its weight, aromatic cedar which has excellent spine qualities. Spine is the stiffness of the shaft and its degree is measured on a spine tester, which consists of a balanced gauge that rests on the middle of the shaft as the shaft is held by supports at each end. A 2-lb. weight is then hooked onto the gauge which then bears down with measured force on the middle of the shaft, bending it to the limits of its resistance. The amount of this bend or deflection, measured in thousandths of an inch, is then recorded on a scale to show the stiffness of the shaft. The weaker or longer the shaft,

In commercial arrow-making establishments, dowels are pre-matched and stored in separate bins according to diameter and weight. Dick Garver, at left, of the Shawnee Archery Co., has only to go to the right bin to select a dozen precision-matched arrow shafts.

As shown at right, necessities for making an arrow include dowel shaft, plastic nock, feathers, and arrowhead (choice of blunt, target point or broadhead).

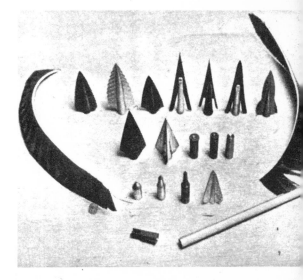

Bob Bennett checks shaft for straightness, sighting along it while spinning shaft with fingers.

Slightly bent shafts can often be straightened by just flexing them in the opposite direction.

the more it will bend. Matched arrows should be made with shafts that all bend to the same degree, plus or minus about .100 inch for a 30-lb. bow and about .050 inch for a 60-lb. bow. Tolerances for intermediate weight bows can be calculated accordingly.

The right spine for your needs will depend on the weight bow you use and the length arrow you draw. The following table can be used as a guide in determining the correct spine for the three most popular arrow lengths. For lengths that fall in between these, use a figure midway between the two lengths nearest to your own.

SPINE DEFLECTION IN 1/1000ths INCH

BOW WEIGHT	26-in. Shaft	28-in. Shaft	30-in. Shaft
30 lbs.	.870 in.	.825 in.	.700 in.
40 lbs.	.650 in.	.625 in.	.525 in.
50 lbs.	.520 in.	.500 in.	.425 in.
60 lbs.	.420 in.	.400 in.	.350 in.

As can be seen from this table, the heavier the bow, the stiffer its arrow shaft should be. Likewise, the longer the arrow, the stiffer it should be. This stiffness is calculated to match an arrow to the bow that will flex just the right amount on release to let it curve around the bow and straighten out properly in flight. A shaft

that is too stiff will fail to bend enough on release and hence go off too far to the left. If the arrow is not stiff enough, it will overflex on release and go off too far to the right.

Besides choosing the right spine for the right weight bow, you also must choose the correct diameter of shaft to fit the specific bow weights. The following table can be used as a guide in this respect:

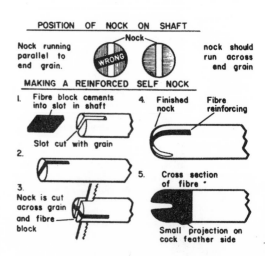

POSITION OF NOCK ON SHAFT

Nock running parallel to end grain.

Nock

nock should run across end grain

MAKING A REINFORCED SELF NOCK

1. Fibre block cements into slot in shaft

Slot cut with grain

2.

3. Nock is cut across grain and fibre block

4. Finished nock

Fibre reinforcing

5. Cross section of fibre

Small projection on cock feather side

ARROW (DOWEL) DIAMETER	BOW WEIGHT
$\frac{9}{32}$ in.	for bows up to 30 lbs.
$\frac{5}{16}$ in.	for bows up to 45 lbs.
$\frac{11}{32}$ in.	for bows up to 70 lbs.
$\frac{3}{8}$ in.	for bows over 70 lbs.

A good way to determine the correct length of arrow for your draw is to hold a shaft with one end braced against the front base of your neck and the other end held between the palms of your outstretched hands. The point on the shaft where your outstretched fingertips reach marks the correct shaft length for your target arrows. Add ¾ inch more for shafts that will be fitted with broadheads.

Another requisite of matched arrows is that they all have the same weight, plus or minus 10 grains. For checking the shaft weights, use a delicate scale that weighs in grains, rather than a postal-type scale that weighs in ounces. Photographic darkroom scales are ideal for this purpose as are the scales sold in archery tackle stores.

Check all shafts for straightness by sighting along them with one eye while spinning the shaft slowly with your fingers. Slightly bent shafts can be straightened by just bending them back by hand, but the more seriously warped ones should be heated a little over a hot plate or stove before straightening. A straight shaft will roll smoothly on a flat table surface.

Once you have separated the matched shafts from the unmatched ones, you are ready to make your matched arrows. The other shafts can be set aside and used for practice arrows. The first step in making

Point where outstretched fingers come together on dowel shaft determines arrow drawing length.

an arrow is to put the nock on the end to be fletched. If you want, you can make your own reinforced nock as shown in diagram, or buy ready-made plastic nocks which only need to be cemented to the shaft. The plastic nocks have tiny raised ridges on their cock feather side so you can tell by feel without taking your eyes off the target how to nock your arrow on the bow when shooting. The bores of these

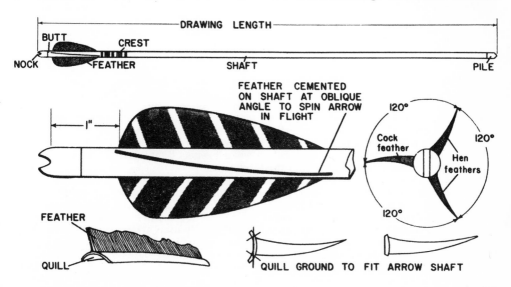

Degree of shaft stiffness or spine is measured on a spine tester. A 2-lb. weight hung on the indicator and shaft bends the shaft to the limits of its resistance. Spine-tester pointer shows degree of deflection in 1/1000ths of an inch.

nocks are tapered to simplify fitting them to any diameter shaft. They are fitted to the shafts by first tapering the end of the shaft with a taper tenon tool, which works like a pencil sharpener but makes a more even and balanced taper, and slipping the nock on with a little cellulose cement to hold it. Ordinary pencil sharpeners, which frequently cut lopsided tapers, should not be used for tapering the shafts.

When putting on the nock, make sure that the string groove is set at right angles to the end grain of the shaft. This is very important because a shaft is stiffer when bent against the end grain than when bent with it, and any shaft with its nock other than perpendicular to the shaft's end grain will not fly in the same manner as the other matched arrows.

If you wish, you can cut self nocks into the ends of the shafts, but these must be reinforced with fiber to prevent the string from splitting the shaft. To make a reinforced nock, first cut a groove into the end of the shaft, ⅛ inch wide and about ½ inch deep. This groove should be cut parallel to the end grain of the shaft. Then, take a piece of ⅛-inch thick fiber and, with cellulose cement such as Duco, fit it into the slot to fill up the slot completely. After the cement has dried, file and sand the projecting portions of the fiber flush with the shaft, leaving only one small protuberance on one side of the shaft. This protuberance will subsequently be lined up with the cock feather and allow you to tell by feel how to nock the arrow on the bow string.

Next, cut the string groove into the end of the shaft, cutting it at right angles to the end grain and the reinforcing fiber inlay, as shown. The string groove should be deep enough to accommodate the string (about ¼ inch) and just wide enough for a snug fit. Flare out the top of the groove to make nocking easy.

At this point, it's a good idea to give the shaft a coat of varnish, shellac, or paint. Any good grade of paint or varnish can be used, and the best way to apply it is to dip the shaft into a container of paint. A special container for this purpose is shown in the photo on page 104. This container is available at archery tackle stores or one can be made by simply soldering a ½- to ¾-inch diameter metal tube to the bottom of a tin can which has a hole cut in it to match and line up with the tube. The bottom end of the tube is sealed off and the whole unit is then used to hold the paint for dipping the shafts. The tube, of course, should be long enough to accommodate the shafts. Dip the shaft, pull it out, let it drain, then hang it up to dry. Hunting arrows should be given dull colors that won't reflect light to attract the game being stalked.

The next step is to fletch the arrow. This means putting the feathers on the shaft. The feathers that have been found most suitable for arrows and are now almost universally used are turkey feathers. Only the two main feathers from each wing tip are used from a single bird. These are seasoned by air-drying for three to four

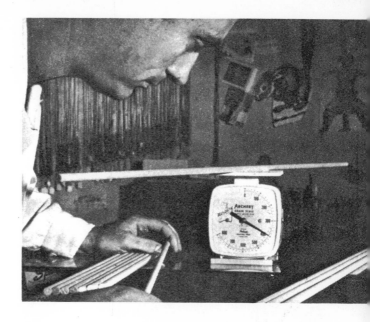

weeks, then washed, if they are dirty, and dyed to various colors such as yellow and red. The quill is then split to separate the unusable narrow side of the feather, and the quill on the broader half is trimmed and ground to a narrow flat base suitable for gluing to the shaft.

Tom turkey feathers are heavier and stronger than those of the hen turkeys and therefore better suited to arrow making, although the hen feathers are also quite suitable. However, since there is a difference in feathers, the arrow should have the same type feathers on it, either all tom's or all hen's. Mixing them on a single shaft will throw the arrow out of balance and affect its flight characteristics. The feathers also come in a right or left hand twist, depending on which wing they were removed from. When fletching, use all right-handed or all left-handed feathers on the shaft. Never mix them.

Three feathers are mounted on each shaft; one called the cock feather being mounted at right angles to the nock and directly in line with the small projecting marker on it, and the others mounted around the shaft, each spaced 120 degrees from the cock feather. The fact that one of these feathers is commonly called the "cock" feather and the other two "hen" feathers should not be allowed to confuse you into thinking that one is from a male bird and the other two from the female. Actually, they are all either tom feathers or hen feathers, never mixed.

Fletching jigs, ranging in price from $1.25

to the professional $12.65 model, are available at archery supply stores and these will take the guesswork and fumbling out of positioning and cementing the feathers to your shaft. It is far better to use one of these jigs and get accurate and consistently matched results than to fletch by hand. The jig not only holds the feather in place while it is being glued to the shaft, but also provides for accurately rotating the shaft 120 degrees to line it up for the next feather.

The size, shape and positioning of the feathers can vary in many ways, and to set down exact specifications along these lines would be almost impossible since individual and personal preferences play a large part here. Some archers like their butts long, as much as 1¾ inches from bottom of nock to rear end of feather, while others, like Howard Hill, prefer theirs as short as ¾ inch. Ted Ekin who does the fletching at Shawnee Archery of Sunland, Calif., considers 1 inch sufficient, which is a good compromise.

In general, it is safe to say that the heavier the bow, the longer and taller the feathers should be. Also, it takes more feathers to balance a broadhead than a target arrow. Likewise, a field or roving arrow which has a heavier field point. Longer arrows also take longer feathers, though not necessarily taller. The following dimensions can serve as a basic guide in determining the best feather dimensions for your own needs. For a 30- to 35-lb. bow, a feather 3½ inches long by $\frac{7}{16}$ inch tall will work well on a target arrow. For a

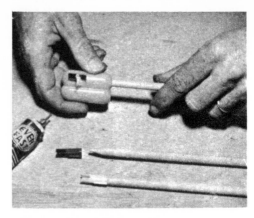

Plastic nock is fitted to shaft with glue after tapering end of shaft with a taper tenon tool.

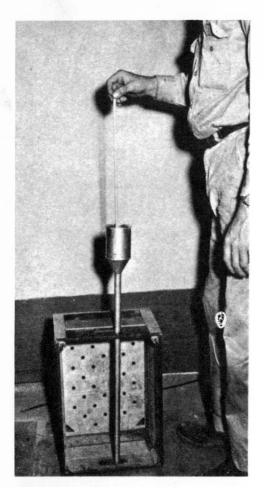

Arrow shaft can be coated with paint or varnish by dipping in container made from pipe and can.

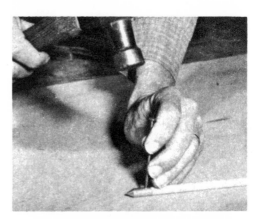

Target or other type point is anchored securely to shaft by denting pile slightly with a nail.

broadhead, make it 4 inches long by $\frac{9}{16}$ inch tall. Add ½ inch to length only of feathers for shafts over 26 inches. On a 40- to 45-lb. bow, the feathers of a target arrow should be 4¼ inches long by ½ inch tall, while for a broadhead, they can be 5 inches long by $\frac{9}{16}$ inch tall. For a 60-lb. bow, add ¼ inch more to the length.

Feathers can be glued to the shafts in a straight line or on a slight diagonal line to make the arrow spin in its flight. Spinning in flight makes for a straighter flying arrow, and this is essential with broadheads to keep them from windplaning. Target or field arrows don't require spiral fletching as much as the broadheads and these can be fletched more or less in a straight line. As a general rule, larger feathers and more spiral for broadheads, shorter feathers and less spiral for target arrows.

The best way to trim the feathers down to shape after they have been cemented in place is to burn the excess away with a hot wire. Feather burner kits to make the trimmer shown in the photos can be bought for as little as $2.50 and easily assembled on a wooden base. More elaborate transformer models come as high as $14.95. Basically, these are electrical devices operating on 110 volts and consist of a nichrome wire bent to the shape to which the feather is to be trimmed and are wired in series with a heating element resistor. When turned on, the nichrome wire becomes red hot and all that is necessary to trim the feathers is to rest the shaft on the brackets with one feather under the hot wire, then rotate the shaft on the brackets to bring each feather in turn up against the hot wire which will then burn it off

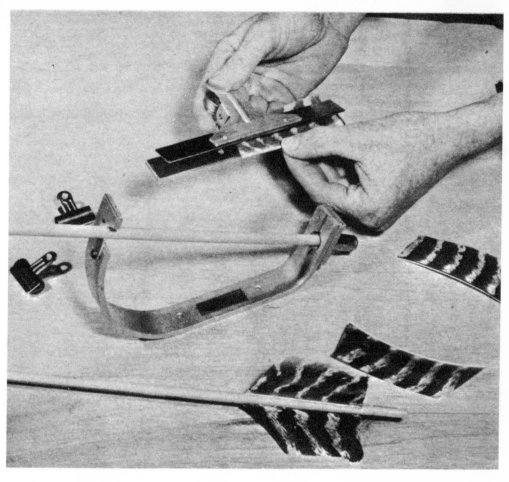

Fletching jigs take the guesswork and fumbling out of positioning and cementing feathers to shaft, hold feather in place during gluing, provide for accurately rotating shaft to line up for next feather.

Cellulose cement is applied in a narrow film to the curved base of feather held in a jig clamp.

Clamp is then slipped into bracket of fletching jig to hold cemented feather in place until dry.

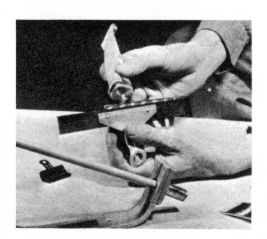

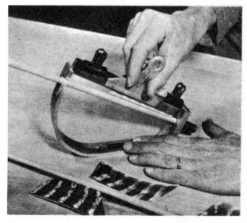

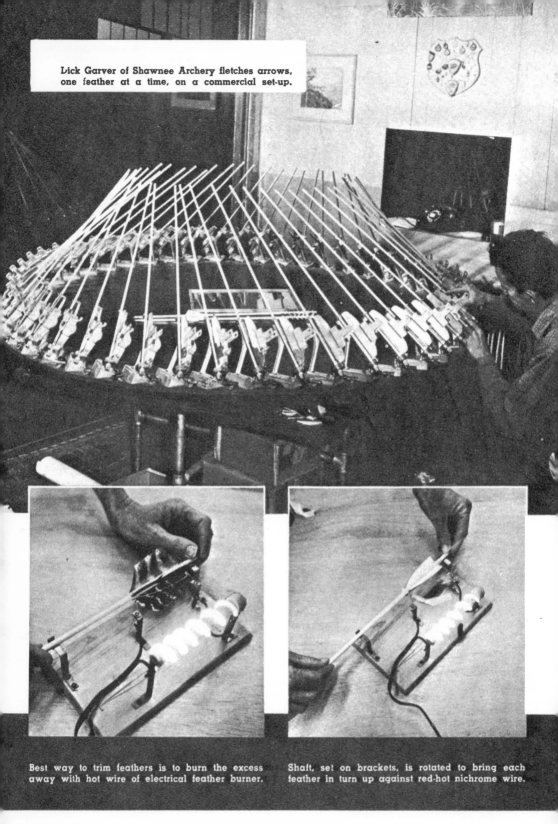

Best way to trim feathers is to burn the excess away with hot wire of electrical feather burner.

Shaft, set on brackets, is rotated to bring each feather in turn up against red-hot nichrome wire.

neatly to shape. This whole operation should be done quickly and without hesitation, for if the feather is allowed to heat up before it is trimmed, there is danger of it catching fire on contact with the hot burn-off wire.

After trimming the feathers, taper the leading edges down until they blend with the shaft, using a razor-sharp knife or a small hand grinder as shown. The charred edges of the feathers should also be cleaned smooth with the hand grinder or a small piece of sandpaper.

All types of arrowheads are available for the various fields of archery and these are easily attached to the shaft by slipping them over the shafts and anchoring them in place by denting the pile slightly with a nail. For those points which have tapered bores, the shaft end will have to be tapered to fit with the taper tenon tool.

If you want, you can anchor the points even more securely by drilling a tiny hole through the pile and shaft and driving a flush-fitting brad through it, then filing the ends flush with the pile.

Finally, you can finish the arrow off by adding a touch of distinction to it, the crest. This is a band of bright colors painted around the shaft, usually back toward the feathers. The colors add a decorative touch to the arrow and serve to identify them as yours, a necessity when shooting in competition with other archers. The choice of color combinations is up to you and, once decided upon, should be duplicated exactly on all your arrows. This will be your trade-mark.

A quick and accurate way to crest arrows is to set the shaft in a motor-driven device that will rotate it while you apply the brush to its surface. A small geared-down electric motor, its shaft fitted with a metal tube to accommodate the nock of the arrow, will work fine. A metal pin to engage the nock should be set through the metal tube and a curved bracket on which to rest the suspended end of the shaft should be fastened to the work base. To use this set-up, you simply insert the nock of the arrow into the improvised chuck, rest the other end of the shaft on the bracket, turn on the motor and, as it rotates the shaft, hold a small paint brush with the desired color against the shaft, steadying your hand against the edge of the table. A slight touch of the brush to the rotating shaft is enough to apply one band of color. Change brushes and colors for different color combinations. Let arrows dry and they're ready to shoot.

If you've made your arrows right and matched them well, you'll have no trouble grouping them on your target, for each will follow straight and true in the path of its predecessor, provided you aim and shoot the same way each time. If they fail to group, it won't be the fault of the arrows. •

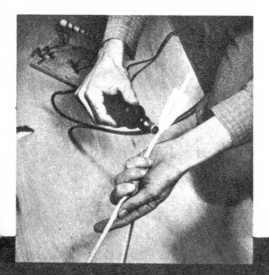

Use hand grinder to smooth charred edges, taper leading edges of feathers to blend into shaft.

A quick and accurate way to crest arrows is to rotate them mechanically while you apply paint.

Care and Repair of Equipment

Treat equipment with respect and you will save much wear and tear —on equipment *and* pocketbook.

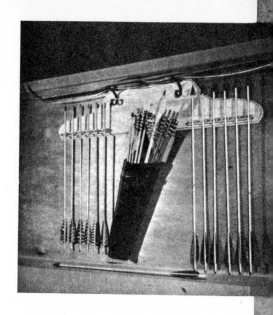

Never store arrows in hung quiver or lay them flat on a shelf. Store them vertically and separately in a rack as shown.

At right, Howard Hill and archer friend Guy Madison go over equipment in Hill's workshop prior to going on hunting trip.

Shooting more than six arrows into a target increases your chances of emulating Robin Hood, but can cost you a good arrow.

YOUR bow and arrows will last much longer and give you better service if you take care of them and keep them in repair. A recurve bow, especially, is a delicate piece of equipment and should be treated with respect, not abused and tossed around like an old cane. Arrows take the worst beating, but there's no need to go out of your way to make things even worse. Following are a set of do's and don'ts which, if adhered to, will save you much wear and tear on your equipment and pocketbook.

CARE OF THE BOW

1. Don't shoot a bow without an arrow in it. Dry-firing puts a terrific strain on the limbs and string and can break the bow.

2. Don't draw the bow without an arrow. You might (1) overdraw and break it, (2) slip and release it, or (3) grip the string too low and overdraw the lower limb, causing it to warp or break.

3. Don't lean your bow against a wall with the tip on the ground. The limbs could warp, the bow could slip, the tips could get damaged.

4. Do hang the bow on a peg or hook (unstrung if you are finished shooting).

5. Don't store your bow in strung position. Relax the limbs before storing it by unstringing it when you are through shooting.

6. Do store your bow in a bow case to protect it against knocks and bruises.

7. Don't shoot with a worn bowstring. If a strand snaps or the string becomes frayed around the nocking point or at the loops, discard it and use a new one. If a string breaks, your bow can break with it.

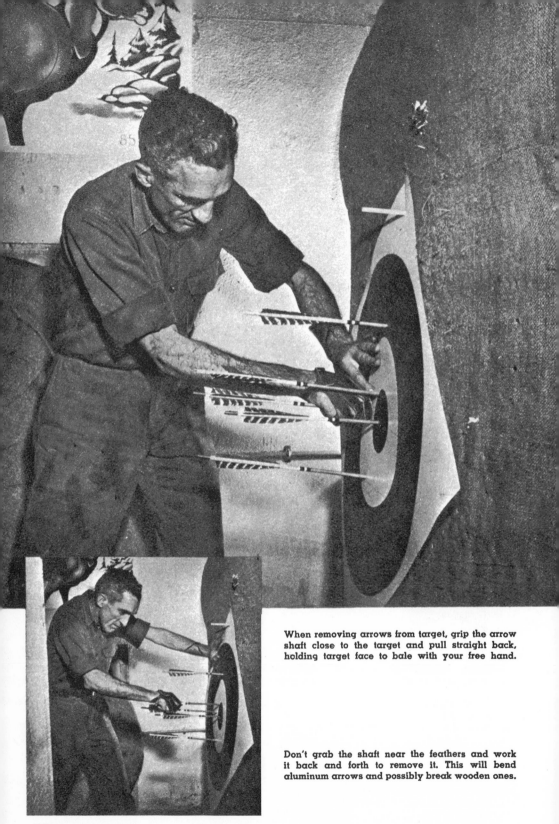

When removing arrows from target, grip the arrow shaft close to the target and pull straight back, holding target face to bale with your free hand.

Don't grab the shaft near the feathers and work it back and forth to remove it. This will bend aluminum arrows and possibly break wooden ones.

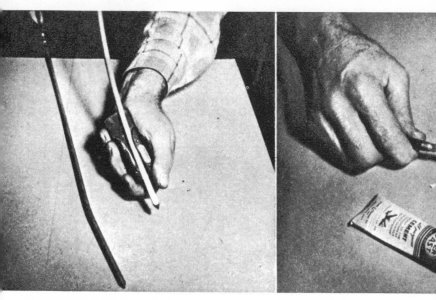

Aluminum arrows can be straightened with simple straightener shown here, designed by Hugh Rich.

Remove broken and damaged plastic nocks with a knife or by burning. Replace them with new ones.

8. Don't use your bow as a cane or staff while hiking through the fields.

9. Don't toss your bow carelessly on the back seat or in the trunk of your car. It should be carefully wrapped in a soft cloth cover and protected from bouncing and being knocked around.

10. Don't shoot an arrow that is longer than the draw limit of your bow. You might overdraw the bow and break it.

11. Do protect the finish of your bow by waxing it periodically with a good grade of furniture polish or wax.

12. Don't drive screws through the bending part of your bow limb when attaching a sight or fishing reel. A hole in the limb, however small, will weaken it. Attach such accessories to the bow with tape.

13. Do wax your bowstring as often as it needs it to keep it permeated and protected. Waxing adds life to the string.

14. Don't step on your bow tip when bracing the bow. This damages the tip and frays the string loop. Do set the tip into the welt of your shoe as shown in the Stringing the Bow chapter.

15. Don't store your bow in a damp, cold, or too hot and dry place. Dry heat will dry it out and make it brittle, while dampness will deteriorate it. Store it where the humidity and temperature are normal.

16. Don't pull the bow to full draw the first time, after it has been in long disuse. Do pull it out gradually, drawing a little more each time and then letting down, until you have reached full draw.

CARE OF THE ARROWS

1. Don't grasp arrows by the feathered end and work them back and forth to remove them from target bales. This will bend aluminum arrows and possibly break wooden ones.

2. Do remove arrows by grasping them in close to the target face and pulling straight out while your other hand holds the target face against the bale.

3. Don't shoot more than six arrows at a time at a close target. If you're a hot shot and shoot tight groups, you might split an arrow and ruin two. You will also damage the feathers by hitting them with other arrows.

4. Don't shoot arrows with damaged nocks. This is extremely dangerous. Remove a damaged nock by cutting it away with a knife or burning it off—then replace it with a new nock.

5. Do not shoot bent aluminum arrows. They can usually be straightened out with commercial arrow straighteners available at archery shops.

6. Don't shoot at targets that are obstructed by tree limbs or rock projections. Hitting such obstructions bend and break many arrows.

7. Don't shoot arrows at tin cans, bottles,

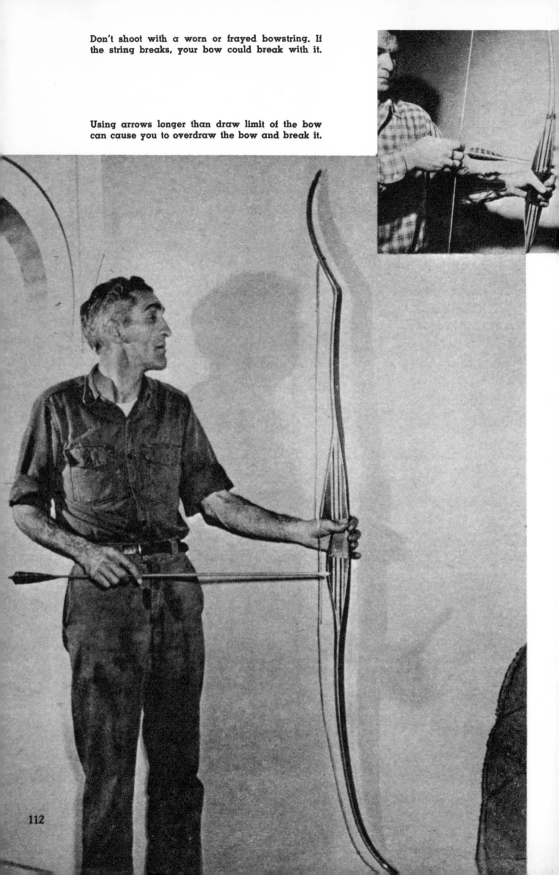

Don't shoot with a worn or frayed bowstring. If the string breaks, your bow could break with it.

Using arrows longer than draw limit of the bow can cause you to overdraw the bow and break it.

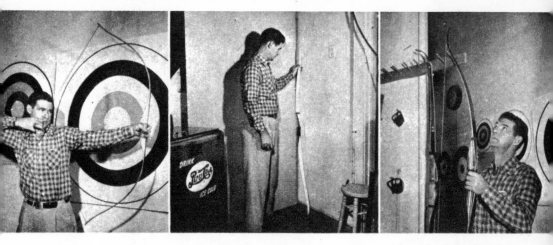

Don't draw the bow without an arrow, as shown at left; you might overdraw and break it. Don't stand the bow against a wall with the tip on the floor or ground; limbs could warp, bow could slip, tips could get damaged. When storing the bow, hang it on a hook or peg, unstrung if you are finished shooting.

or similar rough targets. This will ruin target arrows and damage broadheads. Paper milk and food cartons make better targets for such shooting practice.

8. Don't store arrows in a hung quiver or in a leaning position, or lay them on a shelf. Wooden arrows stored in a leaning position will warp. Bunching them together or letting them lie on a shelf will crush the feathers. Do store them in a rack that holds them in a vertical position, separated from each other. Small clips mounted on a wall are good, or you can make a rack with two layers of hardware cloth, one above the other, to hold the arrows in separated vertical positions.

9. Don't shoot broadheads into sand, ground, or coarse targets. They will become dull and lose their penetrating abilities. Do keep them razor sharp and stored in a manner that keeps the blades from hitting against each other.

10. Arrows that get wet should be wiped dry immediately. Wet feathers that have warped out of shape can be straightened out by steaming them carefully. Keep wooden arrows varnished and waxed for protection.

11. Don't store arrows in a cold damp place, or in a hot dry place. Store them in the same humidity and temperature conditions as described for the bow. •

Protect the finish of your bow by waxing it periodically with a good furniture polish or wax.

Keep your bow in a case when storing it or carrying it in the back seat or trunk of your car.

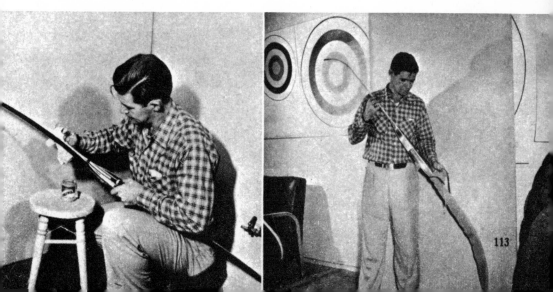

Safety First

Never walk up to a target while others are still in the act of shooting, as Bob Bennett is doing here.

LIVE and let live is a good motto for the archer. In spite of the fact that archery is a family sport, enjoyed by young and old, the bow and arrow is a dangerous weapon capable of inflicting painful, even fatal injuries if handled carelessly. To safeguard against possible mishaps and insure a happy future for your archery, adopt a safety code now and abide by it at all times. A good safety code should have the following rules:

1. Never shoot a split or cracked arrow. It may break and drive through your bow hand. Even a single splinter can disable your bow hand. Watch for tiny cross ruptures in the wood fibers. These indicate weakness that will cause an arrow to break. Such arrows, as well as split ones, should be broken in half and discarded to avoid their further use.

2. Never shoot an arrow shorter than your draw length. You might over-draw it and stab it into your bow hand. If the point should break off an arrow, don't repair it by retapering the arrow and adding a new point. This shortens the arrow and invites over-draw.

3. If a feather comes loose at its leading edge, don't use the arrow until it's been cemented down properly. The loosened, sharp quill can cause a nasty wound in your bow hand.

4. Don't shoot arrows with self nocks (nocks that are cut into the shaft without reinforcement). These are dangerous arrows which can split at any time and drive through your bow hand or arm.

5. When bracing a bow, observe all the safety precautions outlined in the chapter on Stringing the Bow.

6. Make sure your arrow is properly nocked on the string before releasing. A string that slips off a nock can send the arrow off at an oblique angle to the archer, endangering bystanders.

7. Don't stand forward of an archer, even though off to one side. You might become the bystander-victim of a poorly nocked arrow.

8. Don't use a weak-spined arrow on a heavy bow. It can break and drive through your bow hand.

9. If, while drawing, the arrow slips off the arrow rest, don't try to replace it on

Never stand forward of shooter. You might become the bystander-victim of a poorly nocked arrow.

When recovering arrows behind target, set bow in front of target to warn others of your presence.

Never shoot an arrow up into the air, as is being done here It could come down on someone's head.

Don't shoot arrows shorter than your draw length. You might over-draw and stab one into your hand.

Never shoot a split or otherwise weakened arrow. It could break and drive through your bow hand.

Never shoot an arrow that has a loose feather. The sharp quill can easily pierce the bow hand.

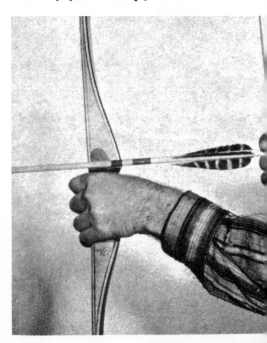

the rest while at full draw. The chances of accidentally releasing it and shooting it through your hand or a bystander are too great. Instead, relax the bow and start the draw again from scratch.

10. Never use your bow hand as an arrow rest. It can be cut by sharp feathers and pierced with small (or large) splinters. If your bow has no arrow rest, put one on it.

11. Never shoot an arrow up into the air. It can come down on someone's head.

12. Never walk up to a target while others are still shooting—and conversely, never shoot at a target while anyone is near it.

13. Never aim an arrow at another person. It's no joke if you slip.

14. In setting up a range, never locate a shooting position behind another target, even though off to one side of it. An arrow can ricochet from the edge of the target bale and endanger the other shooters.

15. When hunting, never climb up or down a hill holding an arrow nocked in your bow. It's too easy to fall on your own arrow.

16. Before drawing a bead on your hunting target, make sure it's an animal and not another hunter. Also, wear a gay-colored scarf or jacket to identify you to other hunters.

17. Watch for fatigue cracks in aluminum bows. Under the constant stresses of archery, aluminum tends to crystalize and bows made of it can break suddenly and snap back in the archer's face.

18. When setting up a home target range, make sure that the target is backed up by a wall, hillside, or the side of a barn, to stop arrows that miss the bale. Never set a target where misses can travel into a neighboring yard or street.

19. On an indoor range, there should be no open doorway where a person could enter into the line of fire. Any such doors should be securely locked and posted with danger signs. •

In setting up a range, never locate a shooting position behind another target, even though off to one side of it. An arrow could ricochet from the edge of the target bale and endanger the other shooters.

Quiver for hunting attaches to bow, holds three broadhead arrows ready in special clip brackets.

Simple quiver of heavy leather slips into back pocket, holds half dozen or more target arrows.

Archery Accessories

Left to right: low-priced belt quiver; flat, back quiver; back quiver with pocket for accessories.

Finger tabs and arm guards, made by King—musts for the protection of drawing fingers, bow arm.

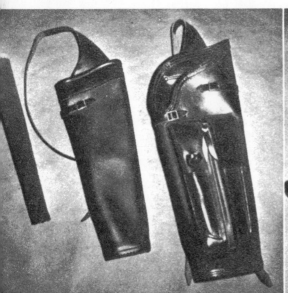

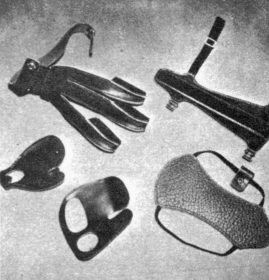

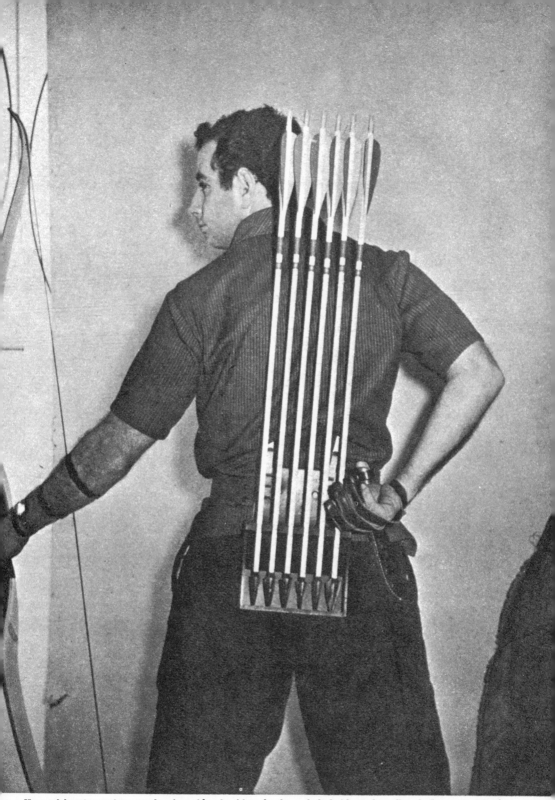

Howard hunting quiver, made of semi-hard rubber, hooks on belt, holds six broadheads flat against back.

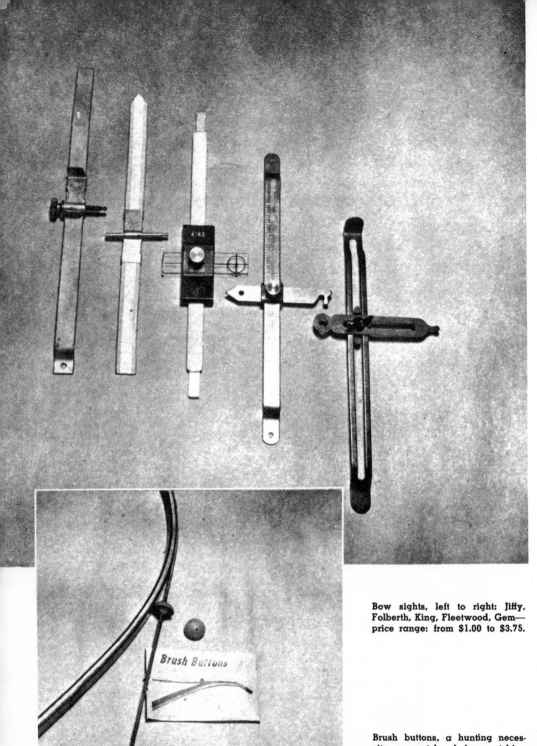

Bow sights, left to right: Jiffy, Folberth, King, Fleetwood, Gem—price range: from $1.00 to $3.75.

Brush buttons, a hunting necessity, prevent brush from catching between bow tips and bowstring.

Bow lock or archery trigger eliminates need for finger tabs or gloves, permits a smooth release.

The device is held in the drawing hand and the string is anchored over a hook-like projection.

Bowstring is held in place on small hook of bow lock by pressure exerted by the archer's thumb.

Release is made by relaxing holding pressure of the thumb, letting the string roll off the hook.

All field ranges should have an area set aside for practicing so that archers can "warm up" before going into actual competition on the range.

At right, Jo McCubbins looses some practice arrows at a practice bale, to check bow and draw.

Games and Ranges

Roving ranges and other competitive field courses test the bow hunter's skill, provide good practice for all archers.

ARCHERY may have long since perished on the battlefield, but as a sport it will never die. Each year, thousands of new enthusiasts join the ranks of bow hunters and target archers to compete for trophies on the ranges and for wild game in the fields and forests. In the early days, when archery first became a competitive sport, target archery was the big thing. Targets were set at predetermined distances and archers competed for high scores. As was inevitable, however, more and more archers turned to bow hunting—and they soon found that the skills they had developed on the range were not showing the same results when pitted against wild life in the field. Having developed their skills with fixed targets at known distances, they were at a disadvantage when faced with live targets at unpredictable distances.

As a natural consequence, a new type of practice was sought, and "stump" shooting, the forerunner of the roving range, was born. This was a very informal type of contest where a small group of archers would wander through a field seeking targets at which to shoot. One might stop and say, "Let's shoot at that stump over there," and that would be the target for the moment, each archer trying to gauge the distance and hit the mark instinctively. The next target might be a leaf, or a piece of paper, or a dirt clod—anything that offered a challenge. This type of shooting proved much more beneficial in preparing the archer for bow hunting, and today, most of the games and tournaments are designed along similar lines, to recreate as much as possible the hunting conditions of the archer. This is the aim of the National Field Archery Association of Redlands, California, which has worked out a series of rounds and tournaments to put the instinctive archers through their paces, while

With two or more targets mounted on bale, archers can take turns getting in practice rounds.

Jo shoots at target through growth of eucalyptus trees on field range; good practice for hunters:

Paired targets save the archers' having to clear the target after every half dozen or more shots.

Every course should have a "29th target," a midway rest area where archers can get refreshment.

at the same time giving the sight users a chance to compete in their own class, the Free-Style Division. More detailed information as to rules and specifications of the various tournaments can be had by writing to the NFAA, Box 388, Redlands, Calif. Briefly, these are some of the games and contests you can set up for your archery practice and enjoyment:

The Roving Range

A series of targets set around a field, each at various (unmarked) distances from the shooting line. Fourteen or 28 targets in all are used (if 14, the course is covered twice around to make 28 shots) and four different sized target faces are used. Twelve-inch faces are used for 15, 20, 25 and 30-yard targets; 18-inch faces for 40, 45 and 50-yard targets, and 24-inch faces for 55, 60 and 65-yard targets. Four arrows are shot at each distance. In addition, the following four position shots are made, each arrow to be shot from a different position or at a different target: 35 yards at 18-inch target, all from the same distance, but from different positions or at different targets; 30, 35, 40 and 45 yards at 18-inch target; 50, 60, 70 and 80 yards at 24-inch target; 20, 25, 30 and 35 yards at 6-inch target. A five per cent variation in distance is

permitted where necessary because of terrain. All shortages, however, must be made up on another target in the same unit, a unit being a 14-target course. In laying out the course, any order may be used as the official shooting order on any four-position shot.

Specifications for the target faces used are as follows: The 24-inch face should have a 12-inch center bull and a 4-inch spot; the 18-inch face should have a 9-inch center bull and a 3-inch spot; the 12-inch face should have a 6-inch center bull and a 2-inch spot; the 6-inch face should have a 3-inch center bull and a 1-inch spot.

The outside ring should be black, the bull white, and the spot black. Animal targets bearing these official round faces may be used. However, the face need not be painted, only outlined, but the aiming center or spot must be plainly visible. The spot must be of a color sharply contrasting with the target color.

Archers can shoot in groups of three to five, four being preferable, with a target captain and two scorers assigned to each group. The target captain orders the shooting at the target and settles all local disputes concerning arrow values.

Each archer shoots four arrows at each of the 14 target layouts in a unit. In 10

Bob Bennett, who instructed Jo in archery, gives her a few tips on her form as she shoots course.

Hunting conditions are recreated as much as possible on this Ontario, California, field range.

cases, this will mean shooting the four arrows from a single post (shooting position) at a single face. In the other four, it may mean either shooting one arrow from each of four posts at a single face, or shooting all four arrows from a single post but at four separate faces. Arrows remain in the targets until withdrawn by the target captain or his deputy in the presence of the scorers. No one approaches the target until all archers in the group have finished shooting.

The scoring is five points for a bull's-eye, including spot, and three for the outer circle. An arrow cutting two rings is scored as being in the ring of greater value. The outer line of the field archery target is considered outside the scoring field. A line arrow, including one in the outer ring, must cut the line so that no color of the line is visible between the arrow and the inner ring, in order for it to score the higher point value.

Broadhead Round

This round with its animal targets and sliding-scale system of scoring is more of a measure of the hunting archer's skill than the standard field round, but if set up permanently and used too often, it will become just another round. The best way

to keep its appeal fresh and exciting is to use the round only occasionally and stake it out differently each time. This round can be staked out on a regular field course to add variety and excitement to the shooting program.

The round consists of 28 targets set at distances varying from 10 to 60 yards, the average being 30 yards, or a total distance for the course of 840 yards. To make this round a test for the hunting archer's skill, the shooting positions should be arranged to force the archer to make a number of tricky shots, such as kneeling, crouching, sitting, etc. Shots set up where the archer must shoot under low-hanging limbs, over shrubbery, between trees, with bow canted to an angle of 45 degrees, etc., will give him the type of practice he needs for actual hunting.

The targets for this round are life-size animal targets with the scoring areas divided into two parts. The center one is a circle around the heart area, varying in size up to 12 inches and invisible from the shooting position. Another area includes all of the animal except ears, horns, tail and legs. The targets vary in size and should be set up with the larger ones on the more distant ranges.

A hit with the first arrow that touches

In range competitions, archers can shoot at running-game targets, good practice for bow hunters.

Archers are required to shoot through trees and from a variety of positions to test their skill.

inside the circle scores 20 points. A first arrow hit outside the bull's-eye counts 15. With the second arrow, a bull is 15 and a hit is 10. With the third arrow, a bull is 10 and a hit is five. A maximum of three shots for each target is allowed, but an archer stops as soon as he scores a hit, shooting no more arrows after that. Arrows must be equipped with a broadhead that measures at least ⅞ inch in width and has a cutting edge at least 1½ inches long. Ladies' arrows must be at least ¾ inch wide with a 1½-inch long cutting edge.

Hunter's Round

This is a round of unknown distances and, like the Broadhead Round, should not be used so often that an archer can become familiar with the distances in terms of bow sighting and thus defeat the purposes of the round.

The target has an all-black background. The cardboard should be 25 inches for all 24-inch targets, leaving a half-inch skirt all around to clearly identify near misses. This face size is used for all targets 45 yards and over. Below 45 yards, to and including 15 yards, use a 19-inch face with an 18-inch scoring area for 35 and 40 yards, and a 12-inch scoring area for 15, 20, 25 and 30 yards. Use 10 or 12-inch faces with a 6-inch scoring area for the bird shots. All targets must have a pencil-lined bull's-eye, half the diameter of the scoring area, and a white aiming spot in the exact center. This spot is customarily four inches in diameter on the 24-inch targets, three inches on the 18-inch targets, 2 inches on the 12-inch

targets, and one inch on the 6-inch targets, but this may be varied if desired since the spot has nothing to do with the scoring. All distances refer to the standard field round and not to the actual distances shot in the Hunter's Round, which are unknown and varied.

The distances of the shots are arrived at as follows: Using red, white, and blue stakes, stake the Field Round out first with white stakes, the Broadhead Round with blue stakes. Then take a handful of red stakes, stand about halfway between the white and the blue stakes, and drive the red stakes at random. In some instances, on the short shots, a red stake may appear to be farther back than the white stake because of the four positions. All of the long shots, say between 55 and 70 yards, should be two-position and identified by a single red stake. You shoot two arrows from each side of the stake.

For the medium distances, 30 to 50 yards, set two stakes for a four-position shot, the archer to shoot one arrow from each side of each stake. These two stakes should be at different distances from the target, sometimes being walk-ups and sometimes walk-backs.

On targets 30 yards and under, use four stakes. One arrow is shot from each stake, staggered in every conceivable way.

Scoring is the same as in the field round.

Battle Clout

This is a game wherein the arrows are shot high in the air to drop them on a large target set out on the ground 200 yards

Jo McCubbins and Leslie Speaks collect trophies after Orange Belt Shoot for instinctive archers.

away. The target has a 12-foot diameter center with rings six feet wide. Arrows must have broadheads not less than 7/8 inch wide and weigh 425 grains or more. Thirty-six arrows are shot in ends of six and the scoring is nine points for the center bull's-eye with the rings scoring seven, five, three, and one point respectively. A bow with good cast is necessary for clout shooting because of the distance involved.

Hit and Drop Back

This is shot on a standard field course under official rules, except that whenever an archer makes a hit, he must drop back three paces before shooting his next arrow. This round is quite an equalizer because the better shot is handicapped by having to make his later shots from greater distances, often finding himself in difficult terrain to boot before he's shot his fourth arrow.

Archery Golf

Some archers actually play this game on a regular golf course and often in competition with golfers, giving the golfers a handicap and scoring in the same manner as golf. They use three arrows: a flight arrow, an "approach" arrow, and a "putting" arrow. The object is to complete the course in the least number of shots. The final shot at each hole does not require the archer to shoot the arrow into the cup but to hit a small ball or disc placed right beside the cup.

A regulation golf course, however, is not essential to play this game for, as the Na-

tional Field Archery Association points out, a good course can be laid out in suitable terrain as follows:

Use a handful of stakes, either painted white or with flags attached, to mark the shooting positions or "tees" and the target locations. The course should consist of 18 targets and the range should be well mixed, everything from 30 to 300 yards. Where possible, put the target markers on knolls, or near the edge of banks, where a miss means a long shot back.

All archers shoot one arrow from tee toward target. In each succeeding shot, the archer whose arrow is farthest from the target shoots first. A hit is scored only when the ball is knocked from its stand, or when the arrow has dropped within its own length of the target stand. All shots after the first tee-off shot are made from the spot where the previous arrow landed. In case of a lost arrow, one point is added to the contestant's score and his next shot must be made from as near as possible to the point where the arrow was lost.

Flight Shooting

This is a phase of archery that stands in a class by itself and is not as popular as other competitions because of the expense and special equipment involved. The flight archer is not interested in marksmanship —only distance—and will go to any lengths to achieve his goal. He uses a special bow that is used only for flight shooting, and lightweight flight arrows that are usually barreled and fletched for flight.

Flight shooting is divided into two classes, regular and free-style. In the first class, the bow is held in the hand and shot in the conventional manner, while in the free-style, more drastic measures are permitted. The most popular free-style technique is to use a foot bow, the archer lying on his back and holding the bow with his feet placed in stirrups on either side of the arrow rest. This allows him to use both hands for drawing and enables him to draw bows up to 200 pounds and more. An example of how far an arrow can be shot by this method is the record 719.6-yard shot by Paul Berry in 1949.

Target Archery

Long before field archery captured the ardor of the hunt-bent archer, target archery, under the auspices of the National Archery Association of Amherst, Massachusetts, was the popular mainstay of organized archery. Unlike the field archer who welcomes obstacles in his shooting sport so he will be better prepared for

hunting, the target archer prefers to shoot under well-regulated conditions at targets of known height and distance, and with whatever mechanical shooting aids he can utilize to better his score. With him, a bow sight is a must, and the archer who can come closest to operating like a shooting machine is the one who takes the trophies. Both men and women compete in some of the rounds, while others are restricted to either men or women only. Following are Target Rounds as sponsored by the National Archery Association:

American Round

Both men and women compete in this one. Ninety arrows in all are shot: 30 at 60 yards, 30 at 50 yards, and 30 at 40 yards. Top possible score for this round is 90-810, the first figure denoting the number of scoring hits made on the target face, and the second figure representing the total score.

York Round

Only men in this one. The York is about the roughest round of all. Each archer shoots a total of 144 arrows: 72 at 100 yards, 48 at 80 yards, and 24 at 60 yards. Top possible score for this round is 144-1296.

National Round

For women and junior girls only. Seventy-two arrows in all are shot: 48 at 60 yards, and 24 at 50 yards.

Columbia Round

For women, intermediate and junior girls. Seventy-two arrows in all are shot: 24 at 50 yards, 24 at 40 yards, and 24 at 30 yards.

Junior American Round

For intermediate boys and girls. Total of 90 arrows shot: 30 at 50 yards, 30 at 40

Flight shooting does not call for marksmanship, only the ability to send arrow a great distance.

Courses laid out over rough, uneven terrain will bring out only the most enthusiastic of archers.

yards, and 30 at 30 yards. Standard-face targets are used.

Junior Columbia Round

For boys and girls. Standard-face targets set at 40, 30, and 20 yards. Twenty-four arrows are shot at each target, making a total of 72 arrows in all.

Hereford Round

For junior boys. Standard-face targets used. One hundred forty-four arrows shot: 72 at 80 yards, 48 at 60 yards, and 24 at 50 yards.

In conclusion, a few pointers about the field range. The ideal field range is one that embodies all the beauty and elements of nature. It is a place where you would enjoy spending the day, even if you weren't an archer. At least 10 acres are needed for a 14-target range, 20 or more for a full course of 28 targets. Wooded hills with streams, ravines and open areas are ideal, but not easy to find. Sometimes a public park that is unsuited to other sports and not in popular public use can be obtained. If the city insists that the range be open to the public, it should help build it, too. Often, the owner of some suitable property that he has no immediate use for can be induced to lease or lend it to your club for a range.

The course should have a central point for headquarters, pleasant areas for picnic lunches, and a spot, midway along the course, where archers can rest and have refreshments—a "29th target" so to speak.

The target butts should be laid out to take advantage of the terrain and provide as much variety as possible for each shot. Have some targets uphill, some downhill, and some level if possible. Shooting across obstacles like streams, ravines and fallen trees makes good practice for later hunt-

ing. Don't, however, go overboard in the obstacle department, for if you make it too tough, you may wind up being the only one left shooting the course after a few months. Make the trails leading to and from the various targets easy to follow. Remember, archery is a family sport, with women, children and older folks sharing the enthusiasm equally with the athletic males, and if your course puts them through the rigors of rough and uneven terrain, they won't stay with the sport long.

While obstacles between target and archer are good practice, these should never at any time obstruct the full view of the target or pose a threat to the arrow in its flight. Although the hunting archer will have frequent occasion to shoot through a hole in the foliage and take a chance on a twig or branch deflecting his arrow in flight, such chances are neither necessary nor desirable on the field range. The path of the arrow's trajectory to the target should be unobstructed by twigs, branches or any other obstacle that might deflect it, for a deflected arrow on a field range is a lethal missile endangering every other person on the range.

In laying out target ranges, never locate a shooting position behind the line of fire of a target butt, even if that post is well off to one side of it, for it is not uncommon for an arrow to ricochet off the edge of the target butt and go off at an oblique angle to its original course. Trails from target to target should also be laid out so that at no time will an archer walk into the line of fire behind a target.

These basic tips should help you in planning a field course that will provide maximum benefits and enjoyment for archers. More specific details for setting up an approved NFAA course can be had by writing the National Field Archery Association, Box 388, Redlands, Calif. •

Photos courtesy Hugh Rich

Archers (using flight arrows) tee off in archery golf; a regulation golf course is not essential.

The Novelty Shoot

Novelty shoots put novice and hot-shot archers on a more or less equal footing, provide fun for everyone.

MUCH of the fun in archery is in competitive shooting, but unfortunately not all of us are capable of the expert marksmanship that makes champions. Although we can all hit the side of a barn with consistent regularity, the guys who are going to walk off with all the loot are the ones who can put their arrows through the knotholes with every shot. When you're competing with and constantly losing to such hotshots, the competitive sport of archery can lose a lot of its appeal—and followers—unless something is done to give the "second-besters" an equal chance at the prize money. The answer to this is the novelty shoot.

The novelty shoot not only puts you on a more or less equal footing with your hot-shot archers, but it offers a break from the monotony of shooting the same rounds time after time, besides being ideal family fare and a good money-raising club activity. You shoot at still or moving targets, some easy, some hard, and on most of them you win by pure luck, regardless of how good a shot you are, for not until you've shot your quota of arrows do you know whether you've been aiming at the high or the low-score section of the target.

A typical novelty shoot is the one held annually by the Pasadena Roving Archers, a Pasadena, California, archery club. This event, the Pasadena Turkey Shoot, is held just before Thanksgiving Day with turkeys given as prizes. All archers are welcome and, for the $1.50 entry fee, each archer is eligible for the turkey door-prize drawing and to compete in all the featured archery events, each of which awards a turkey to the winner.

In a novelty shoot, everything goes. You can shoot any type of tackle you want, bering is different on all three targets and the target is changed after each round so that no archer can tell his friend where the high-score section is after he's shot his round and tallied his score. On one round, the deer's tail may be worth 50 points; on the next, only 10 points. The contestants do not know, so the best they can do is take a guess and try to put all their arrows in the spot that they think is the high-score area, or they might put arrows into three or four different areas in hope of hitting a high-score average by luck. Naturally, the one whose hits total the highest point score wins the prize, and the novice has just as good a chance at winning as does the crack shot.

Another event of this type, but with the high-score sections known to the archers before they shoot, is the turkey target competition. However, even though the contestants *know* where to put the arrows to score, they have very little control in this department because they cannot use their own arrows. Instead, they must use floo-floos provided by the sponsoring club. These spirally fletched bird arrows will not shoot straight. The archer never knows just where he's going to hit, so if he lands in the high-score section, it's pure luck.

The pendulum target is another "lottery-type" competition which changes values with each round. The target consists of a metal pendulum which, when set into motion by hand, swings back and forth in front of a target whose colored target areas fan out from a center point at the top where the pendulum pivot point is mounted. These areas are colored red, yellow and blue. Along the shaft of the pendulum are numbers, spaced about one-half inch apart. One of these numbers, depending on where the arrow hits, becomes the multiplying factor which increases the basic score of the archer. It works like this:

The archer shoots an arrow into the target while the pendulum is swinging. The pendulum then comes to rest against the arrow shaft and the number on the pendulum which lines up with the arrow shaft becomes that archer's multiplying number. The archer then shoots three arrows into the target, aiming for whatever color patch he feels is rated the highest pointwise (this rating changes with each round). He might shoot all his arrows into one color, or place an arrow in each of the different colors, depending on whether he wants to gamble on one color being the high score, or making sure that at least one of his arrows hits the high score sector. After the first arrow, the pen-

In the turkey-shoot competition, all archers shoot "floo-floos" provided by the sponsoring club. These spirally fletched bird arrows do not shoot quite like an arrow should. Not having the control he would have with a set of true, matched arrows, the archer's score is largely a matter of luck.

with or without sights. There's no regulation governing target distances, but because it is easier to control a large group if the events are not spread out all over the map, and more events can be set up in a limited space if the target distances aren't too great, the distances of the average novelty shoot range between 15 and 20 yards, rarely more than 30 yards.

The real excitement of the shoot is in the variety and ingenuity of the targets in each event. Some are moving, some are stationary. The method of scoring changes with each round, so that no one knows in advance what part of a target to shoot at to get a maximum score. For instance, three deer targets may be used interchangeably in a single event. Each is sectioned off into 10 or 12 different parts and each part is arbitrarily marked with a number to denote its score value. The num-

In a novelty shoot, anything goes. You can shoot any type of tackle you want, with or without sights.

dulum does not have to swing. The score keeper holds three cards, each listing a different set of point values for the colored sections. On one card, the red, yellow, and blue sections might be valued at 35, 5, and 20 points respectively. On another card, the values are 10, 10, and 35, and on the third card, 25, 40, and 10. At his discretion, the score keeper shuffles the cards and then lets the top one set the values for that particular round. The archer's final score is arrived at by adding up the points scored in the colored areas and multiplying the total with the number on the pendulum shaft established by the first arrow.

Still another competition that depends on luck rather than skill is the hidden balloon target. Here, four balloons are attached to a hay bale which is concealed by a blanket of newspaper hung on a wire strung in front of it. The archers have to shoot four arrows each through the news-

paper blind without knowing where the balloons are placed. The one who hits the most balloons with his four arrows wins.

Other moving targets consist of small cardboard discs (paper cup covers) attached to a traveling endless belt which brings them into view above a low bale, then along the edge of the bale for about two to three feet before they duck down out of sight. This is a typical shooting gallery target, but the discs are numbered on their backs for point values and the ones hit by the archer make up his score according to their values. The endless belt consists of a belt running around two large pulleys which are operated by a geared-down 6-volt motor. An automobile battery supplies the power. This type of target requires expert skill in hitting the moving discs, but since you don't know what each disc is worth in points, it's still a matter of luck whether you win or not.

In competition depending on luck, archers shoot through newspaper screen, below, score by hitting hidden balloon targets. At right, in popular moving target re-entry event, with boar target riding down inclined wire, scoring calls for skill.

Another competition that calls for skill but pays off on luck is the spinning bale target. This consists of a bale suspended vertically on a cable and holding two targets, on opposite sides of the bale, one being mounted high on the bale and one low. This bale is rotated at a steady speed, thereby bringing each target into view for a fleeting second. The archer must choose the one he wishes to shoot at, wait for it to come into view, then shoot. Scoring changes with each round. The high target may be of low score value and the low one of higher value, and vice versa. Sometimes the sponsors set minus values on a target, which, instead of adding to the score, will subtract from it. For example, the high target is given all minus values while the low one has the plus values. The elation of the archers who hit high scores on the top target doesn't last long when they find out they were scoring minus

133

points all the time. It's all in the spirit of fun, though, and everyone takes the same chances. The mechanism that rotates the bale at an even rate of speed consists of an electric auto windshield wiper motor to which the cable supporting the bale is welded. The motor, in turn, is suspended from a tree branch by another short length of cable.

An event that is always very popular is the re-entry match. This calls for skill, the archers shooting at a moving target that travels along an inclined cable. The target is usually a picture of a running boar or deer mounted on several thicknesses of corrugated cardboard and attached to a couple of overhead pulleys which ride the trolley wire across the range. Each archer pays 50c for four arrows and shoots at the traveling target. When the attendant has collected enough money to pay for the target, the turkey prize, and leave a little profit for the club, he calls a halt to the match. The archer who has scored the highest up to that point gets the bird. The cycle is then started again to raise enough money to give another turkey away. This event can be re-entered as often as desired, but usually, in order to keep the hot-shots from winning all the turkeys, limitations are set on how many birds any one archer is permitted to win.

Another re-entry event features clay pigeon targets, of the type used in skeet shooting, mounted on a board. Each archer pays 25c to shoot four arrows. For every pigeon he breaks, he gets another shot free. A good shot can break nine or 10 pigeons on his original investment and run up a high score. Here, too, when enough money has been collected to cover bird, targets, and a little profit, the high scorer gets the prize.

Aside from the skill and luck events, a miniature roving target range is set up with large non-standard targets on short courses to make it easy for everyone to hit them.

These are just a few of the possibilities of the novelty shoot. The type of targets you devise and the scoring systems you use can be left to your own imagination. The competitions will afford fun for entire families, give everyone an equal chance to win prizes and keep the field of competitive archery from becoming monotonous and discouraging. They will also prove to be very popular fund-raising events. •

The pendulum-target event is a "lottery-type" competition which changes value with each round. The archer's first arrow stops the action of the pendulum. (Number on pendulum touching arrow shaft becomes multiplying factor which increases the basic score of the archer.) Archer then shoots three arrows into the target, aiming for sections he feels are rated highest pointwise.

Another competition that calls for skill but pays off on luck is the spinning bale target. Archers do not know which of two targets has higher value.

The Crossbow

**The crossbow, which ages ago was the "end-all"
weapon, today provides exciting, modern sport.**

DURING the Middle Ages, the crossbow was the most accurate and deadly of all weapons. Today, the crossbow provides exciting, modern sport. The centuries-old crossbow is a hybrid weapon—a cross between the bow and the rifle—utilizing the mechanics and design of the bow for its shooting power, and the stock, trigger and sights of the rifle for aiming and firing the weapon. It shoots a short arrow with terrific speed and fairly flat trajectory, and requires far less skill to hit the bull's-eye than does the conventional bow and arrow.

Though many states ban the use of the crossbow for hunting game, there are still enough states that do permit it under varying conditions to give the crossbow hunter sufficient freedom in the field. In many cases where game animals cannot be taken with a crossbow, there is no such distinction made for predatory animals, and these will provide excellent targets for the crossbowman. However, since game laws are constantly being changed, it is a good idea to check with your State Fish and Game Commission before going hunting with the crossbow.

The crossbow is basically a short, powerful bow attached to a wooden stock that is shaped and used like a rifle. The bow is either wood, steel, or aluminum, mounted at right angles across the forward portion of the stock. A groove, running along the stock, serves as a channel to hold and direct

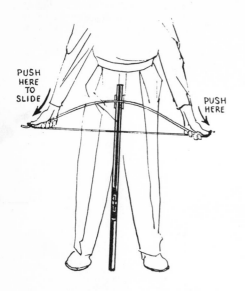

the arrow. The string is drawn back until it locks into a catch that holds it in full-drawn shooting position. A trigger, similar to a rifle trigger, is squeezed to release the string and fire the crossbow. Aiming is done in the same manner as with a rifle, the crossbow being fitted with front and rear sights that are adjustable for distance and windage.

Shown in the accompanying illustrations is the Wamo Powermaster. This crossbow has an 80-lb. high-test aluminum alloy bow, 32 inches long with special re-curved tips for added thrust. It fits into a solid hardwood stock which contains the steel trigger release and trigger guard. An improved automatic lock mechanism simplifies cocking the bow and a spring clip at the rear of the stock holds the arrow in place until it is fired.

To string the crossbow, slip one loop of the bowstring over the bow tip and slide it about three inches in toward the center of the bow. The opposite end of the string can then be looped around the nock or

To string the crossbow, apply downward pressure to flex limbs, slip loops into string grooves.

To cock the crossbow, brace the butt against your stomach, then, grasping the string on either side, in close to the stock, pull back evenly until the string is securely caught in the string release slot.

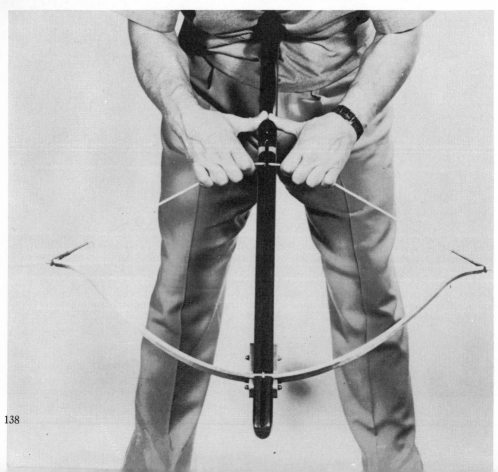

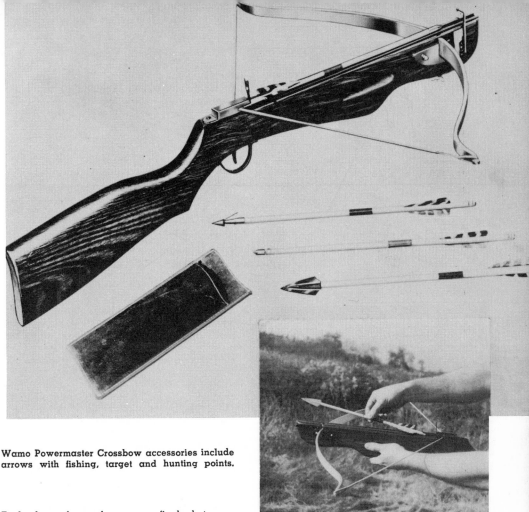

Wamo Powermaster Crossbow accessories include arrows with fishing, target and hunting points.

To load crossbow, place arrow firmly but carefully in track, slipping the back end under the clip.

string groove of the bow at that end. Now, place the butt of the crossbow on the ground between your feet, grasp the bow tips firmly in each hand, one hand holding the nocked loop in place at one end, and the other hand set in position to slide the un-nocked loop out toward the string groove as the bow is flexed. Apply downward pressure on the limbs to flex them and at the same time slide the loose string loop out along the limb until it slips into the string groove at the end of the bow. Make sure that both ends are properly nocked before releasing your grip on the bow and before cocking it. When strung, the string should be 3½ inches distant from the bow at the center. If the string is too long, it can be shortened by twisting it a few turns in the direction of its original twist. To lengthen the string, untwist it a few turns. After shooting the bow a few times, the

string will become stretched and should be shortened to the correct length again by removing it and putting a few more twists into it.

To cock the crossbow, brace the butt firmly against your stomach, then, gripping the string with both hands on each side and in close to the stock, pull back evenly until the string is securely caught in the string release slot.

To load the crossbow, carefully place an arrow firmly in the track, slipping the back end under the clip, with one feather set down in the slot. On hunting arrows, the down feather is at right angles to the hunting head. Your crossbow is now ready to shoot.

The crossbow is held and fired just like a rifle, aiming through a peep sight or notch, depending on the distance to the target. The rear sight of the Powermaster is a

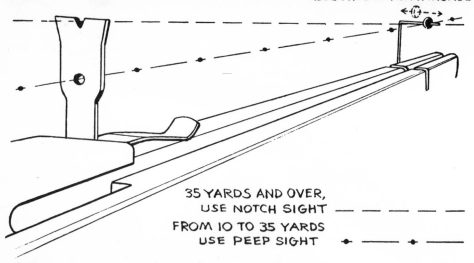

35 YARDS AND OVER,
USE NOTCH SIGHT — — — — —
FROM 10 TO 35 YARDS
USE PEEP SIGHT ◆ — — ◆ —

The crossbow is fired just like a rifle, aiming through peep sight or notch, depending on range.

The crossbow is an ideal weapon for hunting small game, has power enough to take deer and bear.

single unit combining both a peep sight for close targets and a notch sight above it for more distant targets. The front sight has a sliding bead which can be adjusted from side to side to compensate for windage. To aim, sight with one eye through the rear sight, get the bead of the front sight centered in the hole of the peep sight or "V" of the notch sight, depending on which one you're using, hold the crossbow so that the front sight is just touching the bottom edge of the target and fire by holding steady and squeezing the trigger. If your arrows group too high, aim your front sight lower on the target, or move to the peep sight if you've been using the notch sight. If they group too low, switch to the notch sight or aim higher with your front sight. For arrows that group to the left or right, move the front bead sight sideways in the direction your arrows are grouping to correct for the windage. Once you've adjusted your sights properly for a given range, you should have no difficulty in hitting the bull with regularity.

To use the crossbow for fishing, a special harpoon-type arrow is used and this is attached to a line that is in turn looped loosely around a bracket on the stock just under the bow. Fishing reels which attach to the end of the stock are also available for this purpose, but the looped line on the clip has been found generally to be better. For large game fish, the line should be attached to a regular fishing pole instead of the gunstock to afford a better means of landing the fish after it has been hit.

Wamo Manufacturing Company also puts out a pistol crossbow, which is a smaller, 40-lb. crossbow equipped with a pistol grip instead of the conventional rifle-type

To use the crossbow for fishing, a special harpoon-type arrow is used and this is attached to a regular fishing rod and reel to afford a better means of landing the fish after it has been hit.

81041

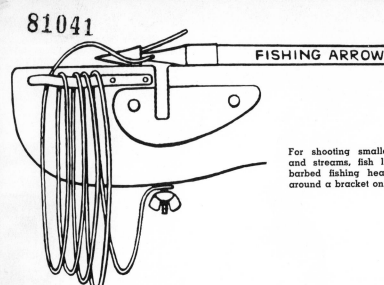

FISHING ARROW

For shooting smaller fish, especially in lakes and streams, fish line can be attached to the barbed fishing head and then looped loosely around a bracket on the stock just under the bow.

stock. This crossbow is fired with one hand like a pistol, holding the arm fully extended and using a rear notch sight and front bead sight for aiming. This small crossbow is ideal for target practice and taking small game and predatory animals wherever permitted.

Unfortunately, the crossbow as a hunting weapon has fallen into disfavor among the authorities in many states, largely through its misuse by thoughtless or unscrupulous possessors. As a result, it is banned for hunting in quite a few states and saddled with restrictions in others. In New Jersey, it is illegal to even own a crossbow. In another state, the archers themselves were instrumental in having the crossbow banned as a hunting weapon. Crossbow shooters had been using the crossbow as a poaching weapon, shooting deer from moving cars and, in many cases, failing to recover the game. To the uninitiated pub-

lic, an arrow is an arrow, and finding wounded deer with arrows in them, they naturally blamed the archers. To protect themselves, the archers asked for legislation banning the crossbow as a hunting weapon.

This type of discrimination can only be overcome by playing the game fairly and adhering to the rules and regulations as set up. Using the crossbow illegally or carelessly will only give the sport a black-eye and bring down further restrictions on its use. Remember that the crossbow is a dangerous weapon and never carry it around loaded unless it is pointing to the ground just ahead of you. For better safety, don't put an arrow into it until you are ready to shoot, and then see that it points only in the direction of the target and never at any other person. Keep your finger away from the trigger until you are ready to shoot. Sometimes, the lightest touch will fire the arrow.

For information about organizing crossbow clubs and shooting in tournaments, write to Col. Francis E. Pierce, National Company of Crossbowmen, 1024 Glorietta Blvd., Coronado, Calif. •

Crossbowmen above, equipped with rifle and pistol-type crossbows, take aim at fish in stream.

The pistol crossbow, ideal for target practice and taking small game, is fired with one hand.

Arrow-shooting slingshot is capable of 40-lb. thrust, making it a very potent hunting weapon.